# A Different Reality

adventures in narrative therapy
& a protocol to address anxiety
disorders and insomnia

## DR. G FREDRIC MAU

WatermarkColumbia.com
Facebook.com/WatermarkHypnosis
Twitter.com/WatermarkCola

## DEDICATION

To my father, George Mau—
Dad, it's been a while, and I miss you.

Dr. Fredric Mau effortlessly blends humor, heart, and intellect to deliver glimpses into his beautiful change work. By sharing his protocols and the reasoning behind them, he gives the reader ample opportunities to start using and adapting them right away. This book is as practical as it is inspiring.

*Melissa Tiers*
*Award winning author of "Integrative Hypnosis: A Comprehensive Course in Change," "The Anti-Anxiety Toolkit: Rapid Techniques to Rewire the Brain," and "Keeping the Brain in Mind: Practical Neuroscience for Coaches, Therapists and Hypnosis Practitioners"*

ॐ৪৩কষ

Smart, eloquent and insightful—with a form of humor that I just love. Dr. Fredric Mau's newest book brings hypnosis and hypnotherapy—and the working and function of metaphors—closer to those on the journey to better understanding hypnosis and its applications. Dr. Mau is always a great read and belongs in the library of every hypnotherapist who takes his or her work seriously. Two thumbs up for Dr. Mau's newest book!

*Hansruedi Wipf, BCH, CI*
*OMNI Hypnosis Training Center Switzerland/USA*
*Publisher of HypoMag.NET*

ॐ৪৩কষ

Dr. Fredric Mau has done it once again. When it comes to understanding something as complex as brain function, emotions and our physical responses to them, Dr. Mau delivers it clearly and with scientific support. This allows the reader insight as to why we respond as we do and how to understand why, in order to manage our responses to life situations more positively and effectively. His vast knowledge from years of research and client interaction allows him to contribute to the understanding of personal development in a way to impact humanity.

*Tom Nicoli, BCH, CI, CPC*
*Principle Visionary*
*Master Visionary Personal Development Coaching*

I am so excited to see that Dr. Fredric Mau has a new book. When I heard it was about the use of metaphors, I was even more filled with anticipation. His use of the English language and his ability to weave in stories and pictures with his words is one of his many gifts. Dr. Mau understands the importance of emotion and how to trigger quick, almost effortless change. With his stories, he will help you to change your own stories and those of your clients. I love listening to his lectures, and being able to read his books continues the soaking in of his skill and knowledge. Plant your seed of metaphors today and enjoy his book.

*Seth-Deborah Roth, CRNA,RN,CCHt,CI*
*Fellow with the National Board of Certified Clinical*
*Hypnotherapists, Specializing in Medical Hypnosis*
*Featured on the Discovery Channel's "MythBusters"*

ॐ৪৩ଔ୫

In his book, *A Different Reality*, Dr. Fredric Mau has put together a series of insightful methods for effective clinical hypnosis session strategies to generate high impact client improvement and long-lasting positive change.

In this work he shares, creates, adapts and improves upon effective use of metaphor techniques, while delineating outlines for insightful approaches into an effective series of step-by-step success blueprints, to boost practitioner impact.

Many practicing hypnotists today will undoubtedly find within this work a highly effective series of tools for inculcating positive and long-lasting strides forward in client personal improvement; these practical insights are highly useful in many areas, including improved stress release and relief, better rest and sleep, releasing blockages, for inspired and better decision-making, and so much more.

*John Cerbone, BCH, CI*
*Master Hypnotist and Internationally Best-Selling Author*
*HypnotistPro.com*

## WHY YOU SHOULD BUY THIS BOOK NOW

"I don't even know why I'm here." Richard flopped down into the chair. It was Tuesday night, the last appointment of the day on a cold, dark autumn evening. He looked miserable, defeated. "I got laid off this week. I didn't even want to get out of bed this morning."

His eyes were hollow. We began.

Thursday night, that same week but otherwise unrelated, and Peter came in: "I've gotta tell you, doc. I got laid off from my job this week."

"Here we go again," flashed through my mind. But I was wrong.

"I always hated that job, but I don't know if I'd ever have had the courage to quit. I'm polishing up my resume—this is a new beginning for me!" The determination was obvious on his face, in his posture. His eyes were fierce.

We began.

You should buy this book because the difference between clinical depression and a new beginning is in the story you tell yourself. You are the story you tell yourself. You emphasize some things, deemphasize others—but change the emphasis and you change your life.

You should buy this book because emotions drive behavior, and stories frame emotion and create meaning.

It is time to learn some different meanings, to consider other possibilities, a different reality.

Buy the book now. You know you will enjoy it.

Also by Dr. Fredric Mau

*Emotion: The Power of Change*
*A Science-Based Approach to Ericksonian Hypnosis*

# Contents

# FORWARD

I am in my office, thinking of Alissa*, one of my clients, as I sit down to write this. Beautiful October late afternoon sun filters through shrubs and spills in the window. I want to write about the power of stories to change the meaning of our lives. I am thinking of the fish. Apparently Alyssa is thinking of me, too; the email shows a new message arriving from her.

The last time I saw her was Wednesday, two weeks ago. We have never met in person; we chatted via FaceTime on my iPhone. I remember she looked stressed. Her father's health is declining, and he had just moved into a nursing facility.

"Every time I go see him, he is so demanding, focusing on minor things, like whether he has enough Depends. I know the man I love is there, but—" she paused. "He's having more and more trouble talking. I can see him suffering. He fell again."

I heard her voice crack. "So much is happening here," she said. "The kids have school, soccer. I just want to isolate, hide away and stay in bed."

"Have you ever been in a pet store and seen the goldfish tanks," I interjected into one of her pauses. I could see her on the small screen; the pattern interrupt

---

*Client stories in this book are true, but names and identifying information are changed to protect privacy.

xv

has shaken her. I saw the confusion opening her to the possibility of new meanings.

"They are swimming and swirling in the big tank, maybe 20 or 50 or 100 gallons. Dozens, maybe hundreds of fish," I said. "But then, when someone goes to buy one, there's that little clear plastic box that holds maybe a pint of water that they hang inside the tank; and someone scoops the fish with a net, and drops the fish in the little box, and the fish goes frantic, darting around that small container, suspended, it seems, in the midst of the schools swirling in the tank."

"I'm the fish!" she exclaimed. A look of clarity flashed across the iPhone screen.

"Perhaps." I said. "Or perhaps your father is the fish. His world has been expansive, but now it's very small. You can see him getting frantic as the world closes in around him. And he's focused on small things. Like Depends. It makes sense."

I saw recognition in her eyes, an almost imperceptible release of relief in her face.

"Are you familiar with Dave Barry?" I asked.

Alissa looked puzzled. "Seems familiar—I'm not sure..."

"He wrote a humor column for the *Miami Herald*," I said. Alissa is pulled in now, thinking of things differently, off the track from the spiral of angst she was in when we started. I could see her interested confusion, the non sequitur of the goldfish. The possibility of a sudden shift in meaning, of real change.

I'd been helping her with anxiety, sleep, pain relief. We'd done the Three Doors and other metaphors in this book. She had a lot to balance, and we'd made real progress. This was a new moment, though. Even through the business-card-sized screen and the ear buds, I could feel the emotion of her change.

I remember flying to Munich for the first time, back while my own father was still alive, gliding across the Atlantic with my 19-month-old daughter Amelia, my wife Sandy, and our 16-year-old foster daughter Jennifer, stifling snickers and sometimes hoots of laughter while I read Dave Barry's book, *Bad Habits*. My wife smiled and rolled her eyes and wished I would be a little quieter on the plane.

"Barry wrote a column called 'A million words,'" I said. I don't think it was in *Bad Habits*, and I'm not sure when or where I read it. I didn't mention that, or the plane trip, or my father to her. This was her session, not mine.

"It wasn't a funny column, but I think it may be the best thing he ever wrote. It's about the last time he saw his father," I continued. "The conversation was something mundane, but that was okay. Barry had shared a million words with his dad, his entire life. He didn't need more for their relationship to be complete."

I could see understanding dawn on Alissa's face. "You know," I continued—and that was definitely a suggestion—"You've told me before you have a great relationship with your father."

"Yes," she said.

"But that relationship is not about hurting or Depends or grief." I said the last word, knowing from what she'd told me before that it was the right word. "Your relationship is about joy. It always has been, right?"

"Yes," she said, and I knew the inoculation is in place. And somehow I knew she would need its protection soon.

"You know, sometimes people have trouble moving past grief. They sometimes feel like it's a betrayal, like letting someone go. And grief definitely has its place. But your relationship with your father has always been about joy. And some time you'll return to that. Return to that joy." I nod, knowing it is a small motion on her iPhone.

I don't consciously recall until later that master therapists value cognitive complexity and the ambiguity of the human experience, and that the life experiences of master therapists become a major resource for them.

"I wonder what you would do differently today with your father if you wanted joy to return to the center of your relationship." I paused.

"And, even though he owns his emotions, of course, I wonder what you might do to help him have more of a sense of purpose now, while he's feeling like a frantic fish in a small tank."

I could see the relief on Alissa's face, the wheels turning in her mind. Our discussion continued for a while, but we both knew the work had already been done. Meaning had shifted, and she was living a different reality now. For the first time, we didn't even do a relaxation hypnosis process in our session.

Now, as I write this, the sky is fading deep October blue to purple beyond the leaves outside. I click on Alissa's email; "My father passed away peacefully Thursday night. I will get back to you..."

Columbia, South Carolina
October, 2014

"People are disturbed not by things, but by the view which they take of them."

Epictetus, *The Enchiridion*

ᏸᎶᏨᎬ

"Denmark's a prison…for there is nothing either good or bad, but thinking makes it so: to me it is a prison"

Hamlet<br>Shakespeare, *The Tragedy of Hamlet, Prince of Denmark*

ᏸᎶᏨᎬ

"The mind is its own place, and in it self can make a Heav'n of Hell, a Hell of Heav'n"

Satan<br>Milton, *Paradise Lost*

ᏸᎶᏨᎬ

"Of course it is happening inside your head, Harry, but why on earth should that mean it is not real?"

Albus Dumbledore<br>Rowling, *Harry Potter and the Deathly Hallows*

ᏸᎶᏨᎬ

"Reason will not lead to solution."

The Cardigans<br>*Lovefool*

ᏸᎶᏨᎬ

"The answers we find are never what we had in mind, so we make it up as we go along."

Nine Days<br>*If I Am*

ᏸᎶᏨᎬ

"Dreams unwind, love's a state of mind."

Fleetwood Mac<br>*Rhiannon*

# 1 SOLUTIONS AND THE SOURCE OF CHANGE

Sigmund Freud believed the unconscious is a bubbling, seething cauldron of sex and death wishes, which probably meant he was a lot of fun at parties.

More specifically, per Freud, that unconscious is the Id, or default unconscious. It did not play very nicely at all with the Superego, or the portion of the personality which embraces social mores and parental guidelines with all the subtlety and gentleness of a Marine drill sergeant.

Stuck in the middle between the Id party boy or girl and the Superego drill sergeant was the poor consciousness, or Ego, caught like a peacemaker child in the middle of mom and dad's abusive marriage.

It is no wonder that Abraham Maslow, of Maslow's Pyramid fame, saw Freud's type of approach as a psychology of sickness. The field was just begging for someone to study healthy minds, with the goal of creating a psychology of health to replace Freud's psychology of sickness.

Milton Erickson had a radically different view of the unconscious. Erickson saw the unconscious as a vast warehouse of strengths and positive emotional resources. In fact—in a complete reversal of Freud—Erickson understood the unconscious itself is the moving force to create positive change.

This is no minor point or academic or philosophical difference. The reality that emotion, not information, drives behavior is critical; emotional or unconscious engagement is necessary for real, lasting change.

## Causes vs. Solutions

So, how do we create change?

Freud argued that understanding the cause of a problem provided insight, which in turn leads to solutions. There is something very rational about this—if we can just figure out what went wrong, then...what?

Clients may get insight, which is wonderful. Except that insight into the cause of a problem usually does not magically fix the problem. In fact, you tend to get more of what you focus on, so if you focus on problems, the problems tend to become worse.

There are exceptions, of course.

Tabitha came into my office. I could see a bit of panic on her face, and hear the tension in her voice.

"You have to help me. It's getting so I can't drive. Every time I get behind the wheel, I can just feel my heart pounding."

"It sounds like this is something new," I said, "what happened?"

"I was in a terrible accident six weeks ago," she began, tearing up as she spoke, and beginning to tremble almost imperceptibly. "I was going through a green light, and this car ran the red and totally destroyed my car. Thank God he hit me from the other side—I'd be dead if he came from my side—and thank God no one was in the car with me."

I asked if she was physically all right, and she said yes. There were bruises from the seat belt and airbag, and she had to see a chiropractor, but no broken bones or severe injuries. I asked about physical pain now, from the accident, and she said there wasn't any. The problem was that she was becoming more and more terrified to be on the road, especially when she came to intersections.

The cause of Tabitha's growing phobia was clear, and fortunately I was able to treat the problem effectively.

The vast majority of the time, however, causes are much more vague and complex—*murky causes.*

Dan, in his late forties and trying to lose weight, was not responding to anything we tried.

Actually, that's not true. We were able to create a number of behavioral changes in his eating habits— dropping snacks, eating more healthy choices, smaller portions— but the weight wasn't coming off.

Eventually I used a regression process with him, when we ventured back into past experiences. Different hypnotists do regression processes differently, and some specifically seek to find causes with the process. As I will explain below, that is not my goal with this approach.

In his regression, Dan went back to a day when he was two years old and playing in the back yard on the swing. He recalled the grass being very green. It was a wonderful, happy memory.

I admit I became a little frustrated during the process, because essentially nothing happened. Dan did not fall off the swing, or otherwise get hurt. There was no problem, and certainly no trauma in the memory he visited. I invited him to visit other events, but he refused. "No," he said, "this is all we need to do. I don't need to go anywhere else."

I brought in a metaphor of an "older, wiser you" to be with him and help him during the regression. This is an invitation to the positive Ericksonian unconscious to step in and create change. The two of them played together, but, again, there was no trauma to reframe.

Eventually, feeling a bit puzzled and defeated, I emerged Dan from the process.

"I don't think I remembered that day," he said.

"Most people don't remember specific, random, happy days from childhood," I allowed.

"Was that real? Did it really happen?"

"I don't know," I said. "Some emotional memory goes back very early, but we really don't have cognitive memories framed by language that early. But it doesn't matter. That story is how your unconscious chose to deal with the weight loss."

I framed the experience for him positively, and encouraged him to see what happened next. No one was more surprised than me when he started losing weight following that experience.

So, what does that mean? Can we say that a man in his late forties is overweight *because* of a random day playing in the back yard when he was two years old? If so, what does that even do to the whole idea of causes? Each of us has had millions of experiences. Tabitha's car wreck was an obvious traumatic experience, but how can we say Dan's day to play was the cause of anything?

Then there are what I term *retroactive causes*.

Tricia, a retired therapist, came into my office complaining of a broken heart. At 70, she had had an affair with a man thirty years her junior. After a month, he broke it off.

"I know it wasn't smart, and that it wasn't going anywhere," she said. "I should never have let myself get emotionally tied up with him."

Then she added the kicker: "Maybe this has something to do with my relationship with my father."

"Wait a minute," I said. I knew her father must have died some time ago (she later confirmed that), and I have helped people heal from broken hearts many times. The key is to reframe the emotions associated with the wrecked relationship; after all, love is a state of mind. "How about if we just deal with your feelings from the relationship," I asked, "and see if that fixes things, before we start exploring things with dad?"

Tricia stopped and looked at me. "If you think that will help," she said.

I did and it did. We were able to resolve her feelings in a few sessions, and there was never a need to explore the question about her father.

However, if she had continued down the path of thinking the problems she was experiencing were about her relationship with her father, she could have created what I think of as a *retroactive cause*. A retroactive cause is at its core a form of confirmation bias, where a client experiences a problem and attributes it to a cause. It does not matter if the supposed cause actually did lead to the problem. At the point the client feels that way, the supposed cause "becomes" the cause, and has to be addressed as if it were the cause. Emotions drive behavior, but stories frame emotions. The stories we tell ourselves create our reality, and if you talk yourself into believing something caused a problem, then for all intents and purposes it did—even if it did not.

More murky is the issue of *false memory*.

Bethany, a woman in her early twenties, came in complaining of depression. But she was experiencing much more: flat affect and, very likely, hallucinations. In consultation with her psychiatrist, we suspected some sort of dissociative disorder.

Bethany attributed her problem to two visits with her pediatrician when she about 8 and with her mother in the exam room, and at age 12, with her father in the room. In both cases she said she was raped by the physician, in the presence of her parents, but they did nothing (her father took her out of the exam room, but took no further action). She said she had only "remembered" these events in the past year, coinciding with the onset of her depression, but that her parents denied either event ever happened.

There is no record of disciplinary action against her pediatrician, whose actions would certainly have violated the medical ethical standards of the late 1990s or any era, and it is unlikely that such events happened. Both parents would have to be involved and consent to the assaults.

We know that trauma victims are more likely than others to experience false memory. It is likely that Bethany experienced some sort of trauma—probably sexual trauma—but the memory is repressed because the actual event or events are even more horrific that what she described. However, if she believes the false memory event to be the cause of the problem, it becomes that in her reality.

In the final analysis, the focus on finding causes is a dark path. Complex life experiences (multiple causes or mini-causes), retroactive causes, and false memories confound the process. In reality, however, the focus on causes does not lead to solutions. A client may gain insight, but the emotions must be changed to create healing. It is also a dark path because this focus is not necessary to create change.

A focus on problems tends to yield more problems. Reinforcing destructive life stories or narratives reinforces the negative emotions. Remember, stories frame emotions, so reinforcing destructive stories is not healthy. It is important to *focus on what you want, not on what you don't want.*

This is one of the genius effects of Steve de Shazer's "miracle question." De Shazer, co-founder with his wife Insoo Kim Berg of Solution-Focused Brief Therapy (SFBT), was heavily influenced by Milton Erickson. His miracle question, to be used at the beginning of the first session of therapy, is designed to shift the client's focus from causes and problems to solutions:

> "Suppose [pause] after we finish here, you go home tonight, watch TV, do your usual chores, et cetera, and then go to bed and to sleep [pause] and, while you are sleeping, a miracle happens [pause] and, the problem that brought you here is solved, just like that! [pause]. But, this happens while you are sleeping, so you cannot know that it has happened [pause]. Once you wake up in the morning, how will you go about discovering that this miracle has happened to you?"

In terms of hypnosis, this is an invitation to *future pacing*, or inviting the client to imagine and experience a successful, healed future. The goal is to shift the client's focus from problems to solutions. It is a very different approach from, "Tell me what's wrong" or "Tell me about your problem."

Simply put, focusing on the past or focusing on problems or causes does not lead to solutions. Focusing on solutions leads to solutions.

**Conscious vs. Emotional**

Reason does not lead to solutions, either. Psychologists distinguish between first order changes, which are surface-level and temporary, and second order changes, which are deeper and more lasting. The goal of therapy, of course, is to create second-order changes.

Essentially, first-order changes are about willpower or conscious decisions. They don't tend to produce lasting change.

The therapeutic approaches of both Sigmund Freud and Milton Erickson are both psychodynamic processes. That is, both hold that powerful unconscious forces drive behavior.

An easy illustration of the power of emotion is smoking. Everyone knows that smoking can cause emphysema or cancer; it says so on every package of cigarettes. No one smokes because they want emphysema or cancer.

Why do people say they smoke? Most people say it's to relieve stress. On the surface, this is a crazy answer. Nicotine is a stimulant; you might notice that people who are jittery and grab a cigarette do not become less jittery. The substance most closely related to nicotine is caffeine. It is as if millions of people believe they need a double shot of espresso to calm down.

It is important to realize, however, that relieving stress is an excellent goal. In fact, people tend not to do things that are self-destructive. There is always some sort of private logic that makes an objectively self-destructive act seem like just the opposite.

The voice in your head that you think of as "you" is called your executive function. The seat of the executive function in the brain is the prefrontal area of the frontal lobe; this is the portion of the brain associated with cognitive or rational processing and thinking.

However, you are more than your executive function or frontal lobe. The brain's limbic system processes information at an emotional level. This emotional processing is non-rational (not wrong or

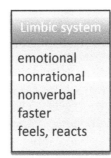
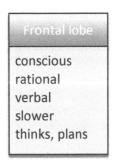

| Limbic system | Frontal lobe |
|---|---|
| emotional | conscious |
| nonrational | rational |
| nonverbal | verbal |
| faster | slower |
| feels, reacts | thinks, plans |

irrational, but simply not conforming to logical analysis), nonverbal, and much faster than conscious cognitive processing. The limbic system—the emotional side, or unconscious—feels and reacts, the frontal lobe (or more broadly the neocortex)— the rational or conscious side— thinks and plans.

Even though a smoker may rationally understand that smoking is unhealthy, at a deep emotional level, part of the person feels that smoking is helpful, perhaps because it feels like it reduces stress. Remember, stories or narratives frame emotion, and the old culture tale (in this case, a lie) is that smoking is the "pause that refreshes."

Body experiences are fundamentally without meaning, but take on meaning and become different realities once we wrap stories around them. The difference between fear and excitement is interpretation; the body response is the same. The stories we tell ourselves are also the difference between feeling worry and concern, frustration and desire, dread and caution, being alarmed or curious, and feeling pressured or courted.

We know that 80 percent of the effectiveness of antidepressants is placebo or suggestive effect. Likewise whether a person has a "good trip" or a "bad trip" on LSD has more to do with the user's expectation before taking the drug than it does with the quantity or quality of the drug taken. That is, the drug causes an experience in the body, but how it is perceived has to do with the setting, the story wrapped around it. In terms of addiction, physical dependence is only part of the story. Psychological dependence is heavily influenced by a cultural, although not necessarily clinical, understanding of addiction that is quite fatalistic and destructive. Our cultural story about addictions is essentially that they can't be beat, which is not necessarily true. The physical feeling caused by the drug is paired with the destructive cultural tale of addiction to become an unbeatable foe, making it less likely that someone will be able to quit.

A smoker who considers the facts and decides to quit is making a first-order, rational change. However, because emotion is powerful and drives behavior, that change is not likely to last. In fact, only seven percent of people who quit smoking using willpower alone are still nonsmokers after one year.

## Ambivalence and Change

Who comes in to my office for help to quit smoking? Not people who like smoking—they just keep smoking. And not the seven percent who successfully quit with white-knuckle willpower.

Externally, smoking looks like a voluntary, conscious act. Smoking does not happen to you. It requires effort. You have to spend money, buy cigarettes, carry them with you, take them out, put them in your mouth and light them up. From the inside, however, the experience doesn't feel voluntary—it feels driven.

Consciously, the person who wants to quit recognizes the problem. The rational or conscious mind says to let it go, for any number of excellent reasons. However, the emotional or unconscious side feels the behavior is helpful. Since emotion, not information, drives behavior, it makes sense that 93 percent of people using willpower to quit will fail.

What we often see in these cases is ambivalence. Ambivalence is one of the key concepts in motivational interviewing. This approach to therapy strongly resembles Erickson's waking state hypnosis in that it does not directly confront client issues, but rather uses indirection, inferred suggestion and questions to help the client create change. When a person is ambivalent (for example, "I want to quit, but I can't"), it's not helpful to participate in it.

If you take one side of the client's ambivalence by saying something like, "Yes, you really should quit—that's terrible for you," the normal result is *reactance*, or to push against the direction: "I know, but I don't think it is really that bad for me."

Being too smart by half doesn't work, either. "You should just keep on smoking. There is no real problem" won't move the needle because the client, of course, recognizes this is emotionally insincere.

In both motivational interviewing (MI) and Ericksonian hypnosis, client resistance is regarded as a failure on the part of the therapist to maintain the therapeutic alliance with the client, not as a client problem or failure. The key to handling ambivalence is to allow the client to own both sides of her or his ambivalence, while making open statements or using open questions that invite the client to see things in a new way.

**Stress and crisis**

Stress mounts up like a wave swells. As I write this, I am imagining Katsushika Hokusai's iconic painting of *The Great Wave off Kanagawa*, Japan, with the monster wave rising up out of the ocean, the sea foam like claws ready to rip everything in their path.

Different stresses roll up into the wave as it mounts. Since they are connected by you, they are not separate issues. If you have a day when the boss chews you out, your dog dies, and your spouse is mad that the bank called and you're behind on the mortgage, these are not three separate issues. They combine in the same stress wave.

Psychologists distinguish between distress (bad stress) and eustress (good stress), although both are the same physiologically. In both cases the body produces lots of cortisol, the primary stress hormone, and you feel it. Stories frame emotion, so eustress is better, but it is important to realize the same physical stress reaction occurs. So while everyone knows that getting divorced or fired is stressful, a wedding is also stressful, as is getting hired or promoted. In real life, you must deal with distress and eustress at the same time—it all mixes and rises into the same mounting wave.

We possess various coping mechanisms for stress— it's how we keep our heads above the water. Some are very effective and productive, some are mediocre, and others are perceived as helpful but are actually counterproductive (smoking is an example of the latter, because it raises cortisol levels).

There are a few good things about stress. One is that people tend to be more productive when we are moderately stressed or aroused. If you are completely nonchalant, you don't tend to get much done. You have high ambivalence and you simply don't take action.

But when stress becomes too high and approaches crisis, it becomes paralyzing. When you are overwhelmed, productivity drops.

As long as the level of stress remains lower than the level of coping, you tend to be okay, although the closer the stress wave comes to your capacity for coping, the tougher it is to keep your head above water. Crisis occurs when stress exceeds coping.

A moderate amount of stress or arousal is the key to getting things done, but it is a mistake to think that you need to surf the edge of high stress to be effective – it's a fast way to crash or burn out.

Another good thing about stress is that you cannot maintain that physical level of arousal/excitement/terror (all synonyms) indefinitely. It is simply not possible. Even if you do nothing, stress will begin to dissipate. Generally this does not happen quickly enough to be satisfying, but it will happen. You become exhausted with the drama.

This is why suicide is always a permanent solution to a temporary problem; stress will subside—it has to. The body only has so much capacity to manufacture hormones like cortisol. Another problem, of course, is that when the body is busy using capacity and raw materials to make cortisol, these resources aren't being used to make other needed hormones, so there can be a double whammy: too much cortisol + too little of other needed hormones. Long-term overproduction of cortisol can even lead the adrenal glands to become chronically fatigued (adrenal fatigue).

There are many ways to create the *relaxation response* to stress and reduce cortisol. Exercise is one, or you could opt for a hot bubble bath or shower, functional relaxation (mindfulness, meditation, hypnosis), massage, sex, or deep breathing. It is almost impossible to worry and take action at the same time, so developing life skills to plan, take action, and accomplish goals is another option. In other words, one approach to addressing stress is to increase your level of coping.

However, an individual can only sustain limited coping capabilities, while the world can mete out infinite stress. Therefore, reframing stress is the primary life skill for reducing stress. As you saw with the two men who were laid off in the *Why You Should Buy This Book* vignette, it's often not what happens to us, but the way we see it that matters. Reducing stress involves stepping into a different reality. It is a fundamental shift in meaning at an existential level.

I am not talking about living in unreality or a delusion. Both men had to deal with the real-world consequences of being laid off; they needed to be able to buy food, shelter, and gasoline. That is the bottom line, but the meanings they created and responses they expressed were very different. One was becoming clinically depressed (which, while a popular option, is not a particularly effective way to deal with stress), while the other was highly motivated by the experience and saw this is an opportunity to create a new life for himself.

Emotion drives behavior. Stories create meaning and frame emotion. We can use story and metaphor to interrupt destructive stories, create a fundamental shift in existential meaning at deeply felt emotional level and thereby develop a different reality.

**Culture tales**

We tell ourselves stories that give our lives meaning, but these stories are not skull-bound and individual. We insert ourselves into the context of culture tales, religious narratives, racial sagas, family stories. As you see in this book, these narratives, long and short, can come from anywhere.

For most of history our social meaning stories have been local or regional. Occasionally something like the *Iliad*, Plato, or Aristotle would break through as a more broadly adapted narrative, but it was rare. After Johannes Gutenberg invented the printing press, we began to share our stories more broadly.

When Charles Lindbergh returned from the first solo transatlantic flight in 1927, an estimated 25-30 million people listened to his welcome-home party on the six million radio sets then in use. At the time, it was the largest shared audience experience in the history of any mass medium. Radio gave way to television, which for a while provided some homogeneity of cultural narratives via three broadcast networks and PBS in the U.S., and a handful of channels elsewhere.

Those days of limited channels are long gone. Our culture tales are again fragmented, but the globalized Internet means people can seek out others with similar stories. New technology in music and publishing allows more individuals to get their message out to an increasingly niche-oriented culture.

So broadcast television has given way to—what? Music is minutely segmented along taste and demographic lines; ditto for books. Organized religion is declining in our society as individuals pursue a more personalized spiritual journey. Internet memes and viral videos proliferate like a springtime snow, flying fast through Facebook, Twitter, Second Life, and World of Warcraft and then quickly melting away (but with a cumulative memory effect over time, I believe). Major motion pictures are perhaps the single medium that still reaches wide audiences.

The use of truisms and clichés to plant seeds and suggest new meanings is powerful. The ability to use current narratives and life tales is key in a world of rapidly shifting culture. An insight from *The Terminator*: "There is no fate but what we make," or *Batman Begins*: "It's not who I am underneath, but what I do that defines me," can be profound—not because these are universal truths (they're not), but because they can be repurposed as catalysts for change.

**Change the meaning, change the mind**

In therapeutic work, I often use *pattern interrupts*, non sequiturs designed to derail a destructive narrative or pattern of thinking on the part of the client. The goal is to create a small amount of confusion, which opens the client to new possibilities. It's natural for people to follow schemas or scripts of meaning; they expect a story to go a certain way, or for certain types of responses to follow.

The goal of a pattern interrupt is to violate that stereotypical expectation and create a moment of confusion in which the client doesn't have a script to follow. In other words, this is a moment of meaninglessness, and a window for change. It creates a transderivational search, an intense mental effort by the client to find new meaning because there is no clear or habitual pattern to follow. Deep emotional change happens in the midst of a quick. thick flurry of fuzzy logic and blurred lines. Since the path is fuzzy, not clear, the client must work to create meaning—to create a different reality.

There are many examples of pattern interrupts in this book. These occur during waking state conversations. In a typical client visit, I don't think of the "pretalk" as perfunctory and the "hypnosis session" as the time for change. Erickson was well aware of the power of suggestion in the ordinary waking state. Change language can be engaged at any level of consciousness. In fact, high emotion itself provides a profound opportunity for change.

In ordinary conversation, the pattern interrupt creates a window of emotional openness in the waking state. Relaxation hypnosis is another way to create emotional openness. Hypnotic suggestibility is associated with frontal lobe inhibition and a deactivation of the executive function, which allows the limbic system, the seat of emotion, to come to the forefront. Since emotion drives behavior, this creates an excellent opportunity for deep change. The emotional part of you is still you, so the change will be yours—but it is a deep shift in meaning, not first-order cognitive redecorating.

That's the value of noting how the stories and introductory materials are used with clients in this book. They are part of the context for the italicized metaphors at the end of each chapter.

**Narrative models and a pattern for the protocol**

This book is designed to accomplish two things. First, the stories and vignettes in the book, like Alissa's story in the Forward, are designed to model a pattern for narrative therapy in the waking state. We are the stories we tell ourselves. The goal of using narratives and pattern interrupts is to get clients to seize a deep emotional and existential shift in fundamental meaning; to help them perceive—not just think about—life differently; to see things in a new way and to literally create a different reality.

Second, these pages provide a structured protocol for treating anxiety disorders and insomnia using hypnotic metaphors in the Ericksonian tradition. Both approaches use stories to help clients edit their own stories and create new existential meanings. So this is essentially a how-to manual for therapists to provide postmodern therapy.

An Ericksonian protocol is sort of like a circular square, a sunlit night, a sensible kōan, or a unicorn. Erickson firmly believed in individual differences, and in using stories which profoundly connected to a specific individual in a particular setting. One mistake people make is attempting to use Erickson's metaphors themselves. Even though stories need to be individualized, I do find there are certain patterns of metaphors that I often use in the hypnotic session with clients. For example, I use some version of The Three Doors with virtually every client with anxiety issues. Below is one possible pattern for a protocol for the treatment of anxiety:

- **Session 1: The Three Doors.** This is a go-to metaphor to begin. It provides a good first experience, and engages the creative, emotional unconscious to produce a wide range of possible changes.
- **Session 2: Fading Photographs.** My approach is solution-focused, not past- or problem-focused. The only interest in dealing with the past is to eliminate past-centered emotions that can be triggered into the present and cause problems now. This process accomplishes that. More experienced hypnotists may use regression (in a solution-focused way, not as an exploration for causes) here, especially if you are a therapist addressing real trauma. If the client is very focused

15

on the intrusion of some past emotion, you might start here, and use the Three Doors next.

- **Session 3: Beautiful Deep Sleep.** Sleep issues are almost always associated with anxiety, so this is a good choice for a third session. If the presenting problem is insomnia, you would start here and then probably move to the Three Doors for the second session.

The other metaphors may be used in additional sessions as needed.

- **The Surfer**. The concept of self-efficacy important to emotional health, so you probably will use this with almost every client. In the other half of this chapter, the Surfer is useful for the client who is struggling with too many overwhelming issues outside of his or her control. This metaphor leverages the truth that you don't have to control everything around you (the wave), you only need to balance your own life (the surfboard).
- **The Muse.** This process is for clients who have trouble making decisions. These could be very focused, or they could be one of life's bigger questions. If a client is stuck on the horns of a dilemma, use the Muse.
- **Beautiful Winter.** In my opinion, physical pain alleviation is the most effective thing you can do with hypnosis. If your client presents with chronic pain, or if your discussion reveals that this is a key problem, you may even want to start here in the first session. The presence of pain severely reduces a person's ability to cope with stress, so pain must be addressed if present. Because physical pain must be diagnosed and treated by a physician, only do pain alleviation after the client has a medical diagnosis. The process is anesthetic, so remind the client to avoid actions that would cause further injury.

## 2 THE THREE DOORS
*a metaphor for releasing stress and anxiety*

It happened somewhere back in our long ago, but the lesson stuck with me: You can learn something from anyone. We were just married and living in San Diego. I was a grad student, and my wife, Sandy, was working on her undergrad. We were both going to school full time, and both working, so (of course) we had no money.

During a rare break from studies, Saturday afternoon found us wandering the Galleria, a posh, upscale shopping mall of the sort you find in southern California—a place definitely out of our economic range.

We passed the windows of one of those chic dress stores that's so exclusive (and apparently so expensive) you never ever actually see anyone in the store except for the salesgirl. We stopped as one of the fabulous dresses caught our eye. It was an exquisite cocktail dress, well-made, gorgeous. I was not surprised by the four-digit price tag.

"It's a beautiful dress." The salesgirl's voice was like silk. "You would look fantastic in it." She smiled at Sandy. She was right, of course.

Since we were eating beans at that time while we saved for a microwave oven, saying the dress was outside our price range was sort of like saying Florida was a little to the East.

"Oh, I love it," Sandy offered. "I just don't have any place to wear it." That was certainly true. We weren't headed to any A-list parties in Hollywood any time soon.

The salesgirl gave a slight nod as she smiled. "We make occasions."

*We make occasions.* I've often repeated the truth of that statement, the power of it. We create our own opportunities, our own power, our own lives. We make occasions.

## The power of imagining change

This process is good for what ails you, or your client.

In *Emotion: The Power of Change*, I presented a version of the Three Doors process as a follow-up session when treating phobia, and it is great for that. The truth is that I use some version of this metaphor with almost every client who comes through my door. Most of my practice is treating stress and anxiety disorders, followed by mood disorders (depression).

The Three Doors metaphor holds power because it invites the emotional side, the Ericksonian unconscious, to image a story of change. Hypnotists refer to this invitation to imagine change as *future pacing*. Often, future pacing involves a fairly detailed process of creating a vision of the future, either as an interactive process where the client speaks while in hypnosis, or in a narrative based on the pretalk with the client.

The Three Doors is different, because it does none of the above. It simply invites the client to imagine the change, which is even more powerful than creating a description of a specific change. Moreover, if the process is recorded for the client, then each time she or he listens to it the process can be about a different topic or issue.

## A process for problems and stress

I see this as a process for dealing with problems, not traumas. The Three Doors invites the client to envision a problematic situation from the past, and to step into it and feel it. With people who have experienced trauma, I use an interactive process (usually a hypnotic regression with a solution focus). Trauma should only be treated by a licensed therapist or qualified mental health professional. However, those who have endured trauma can benefit from the Three Doors; I simply tell them beforehand that this is a process for dealing with a problem, not a serious trauma, and invite them to mentally handle it that way.

## Two key concepts

The set-up for the Three Doors includes two key points. I begin by asking the client, "Do you notice how something happens and you react, and something happens and you react, and something happens and you react, to the point where, whenever something happens, whatever the something is, there is this reaction that just seems to follow? A reaction that has to happen." Almost always the answer is yes. Most clients struggle with being stuck, and with trigger events in the present that engage destructive patterns or emotions from the past.

I then explain that we are going to do a process designed to engage their creative, emotional side, so that when something happens, whatever the something is, they can respond differently – this is the first goal.

I once had a client tell me that much of the time her reactions were not decisions; they just seemed to happen. She took the Three Doors as an invitation to decide to do things differently, at a conscious or cognitive level. Of course it can be that, but the design here is to operate on a deeper, more visceral, autonomic level, so that new possibilities open up at an emotional level, before rational processing comes into play.

Consciousness is expensive. In an adult human about 20 percent of your daily calorie burn is brain function; in small children it is about 50 percent. This compares with about 10 percent for primates and about five percent for your dog or cat. Sensory information constantly flows in. For example, you are not aware of the sensation of the shoes on your feet or the shirt on your back (until I mention it now). That sensory information is processed unconsciously. That's fortunate, though, because if you were constantly aware of those sensations, you probably couldn't stand to wear a shirt or shoes. But if something weird happens—a bug lands on your arm or a mouse runs across your foot—then the sensations immediately become conscious. This is a natural mechanism for your survival and protection.

Incoming sensory information is processed by two main centers. First, the amygdala registers, perceives, and analyzes sensory data very quickly, but at the crude level of gross pattern recognition. For example, you are walking through the woods and you see a brown, wavy form on the ground: Snake! Immediately your body reacts with flight or fight. Adrenalin and cortisol shoot up, you have a startle response and jump back, your heart rate increases.

Then the cerebral cortex, the most highly evolved part of the brain, shows up late to the party. This is the part of your brain that realizes, "wait a minute, that's a stick; I'm okay." But the elevated cortisol and the rapid heartbeat—all the emotional arousal—is still going.

This emotional response can be critical. Jumping out of the way of a snake can keep you alive, even if twigs are not so dangerous. On the freeway a car swerves into your lane, and immediately you check mirrors, grip the steering wheel tightly, lay on the horn, shield your passenger from jerking as you switch lanes, pump the brakes if needed. You won't think about those actions; if you did, you would wreck because the conscious mind is just not fast or adept enough.

Emotions are fundamentally non-rational and without meaning in a cognitive sense; they are body experience emotions occur before cognition processes meaning. The experience of arousal is about engaging one of the three Fs (flight, fight, or sex). These sensations take on meaning as the cerebral cortex comes into play. Meaning is created by the cerebral cortex, but it is not as powerful as the raw emotion of the amygdala.

The first goal of the Three Doors is to engage the emotional unconscious to allow the interrupt to happen at that level, so that an unneeded visceral, autonomic response is avoided before conscious engagement even happens.

The second key concept is this: You own your emotions. No matter what happens in the world around you, no matter how bad things get, you can be okay. That can seem like a trite point, so I ask if they have ever heard of Viktor Frankl.

Many people are familiar with Frankl's name. The Austrian psychiatrist practiced in the generation following Freud. Frankl was the founder of Logotherapy, and one of the key fathers of the Existential approach to psychotherapy. His book, *Man's Search for Meaning*, is a masterpiece.

Frankl was Jewish, and was a survivor of the Nazi death camp at Auschwitz. Frankl was tortured in other concentration camps as well, including ones associated with Dachau, and his wife, Tilly, died in Bergen-Belsen.

In the face of all this, one of Frankl's most famous concepts is summed up in this quote: "Everything can be taken from a man but one thing: the last of human freedoms—to choose one's attitude in any given set of circumstances, to choose one's own way."

It is ridiculously, absurdly easy for me, sitting in a nice office in peaceful Columbia, South Carolina, to say that no matter what happens, no matter how bad things get, you can choose how you respond, you can own your own emotions—own yourself. Viktor Frankl, however, earned the right to claim the truth of this powerful concept because he said it as he was carried out of a death camp.

**Thoughts on anger and depression**

The ability for clients to own their own emotions and responses is critical. For example, a number of clients come to me with anger issues, or want anger management therapy. I've always thought that managing anger is a bit silly. Wouldn't it would be far better not to experience the anger to begin with?

Anger is the default human response to stress; toddlers demonstrate anger with tantrums. If you get angry it is probably because you feel stress.

As adults, though, we learn that anger rarely, in fact almost never, makes a problem better. Responding in anger tends to make things much, much worse. The key is not to manage the anger, but to engage the Ericksonian unconscious, the powerful, creative, emotional side of you, and to respond differently to stress and adversity in a manner that's more effective.

Similarly, depression works like an emotional fire alarm in a manner similar to physical pain. Pain is not bad or wrong; it's your body's way of letting you know there's a problem that needs attention. The pain can become its own problem; it often lingers even after you realize there is a problem (for instance, back pain), or can even begin to loop and persist after physical healing.

Depression should be treated by a licensed therapist or qualified mental health professional, not a lay hypnotist. Particularly if suicidal ideation is present, it is critical to immediately get the client appropriate professional help. Antidepressants, prescribed and monitored by a psychiatrist, can be helpful or even necessary when addressing moderate to severe depression, although they should always be used in conjunction with psychotherapy.

The key characteristic of depression, rumination, is a focus on a problem to the extent that other aspects of life are neglected. The issue is not the alarm, but rather the underlying problem. Like physical pain, the emotional pain of depression can continue even after the problem is recognized, and the habit of depression can continue even if the initiating issue is resolved.

But treating depression can be like trying to turn off an alarm while a fire still rages. Although it makes sense to treat depression (and particularly with severe depression or suicidal ideation, treatment is absolutely necessary and antidepressants as well as psychotherapy can be effective), just as it can make sense to treat pain, the real key is to address the underlying problem—to put out the fire that set off the alarm.

One way to put out the fire is to give the client a tool to handle issues, problems and stressors more effectively. That's a key outcome of the Three Doors process.

ഇൟൟൟ

## The Three Doors hypnosis process

*I'd like to invite you to imagine that you are sitting in a rocker on the porch of a lovely mountain cabin or lodge, looking out at beautiful trees. This is the sort of space where you can just allow your mind to relax, your body to relax, everything to relax.*

*As you breathe you feel the fragrance of the trees, perhaps spruce and cedar and pine, or redwood; perhaps oak or hickory or maple, perhaps aspen. I can't know exactly what you'll experience right now as you allow yourself to flow into this image, but there is a powerful part of you, an other-than-conscious creative part of you, which knows exactly what's best for you, exactly what's right for you – exactly what you need. So you can just let that happen. Let that happen, now.*

*And it may be that you think of yourself as not being very visual, and it seems difficult to try to imagine the beautiful view from that rustic porch now, but that's okay. You can just pretend you are there if you like.*

*And of course there is a part of you that knows how to create that experience, the experience of rocking gently on the porch of that rustic mountain cabin or lodge, noticing how comfortably your body settles into the chair now, the way the chair supports you, beneath your head and shoulders. Supporting you just like your creative other-than-conscious supports you as you blink over 21 thousand times a day, naturally and normally, without even noticing it. Your body is always taking care of you, even as your eyes feel heavier and heavier now.*

*And if you feel you just can't see what's in front of you now, that's okay. Perhaps you will enjoy imagining the gentle sound of the breeze in the leaves of the trees, the fragrance of hickory or cedar or even aspen or redwood; or even ash or sycamore maple, carried to you on a gentle breeze, as you allow yourself to step into that experience and breathe it in now.*

*I am not even sure if you can hear the gentle babble of a mountain stream in the background—if your powerful creative other-than-conscious is powerful enough to create that. And I wonder just how powerful your powerful other-than-conscious is, as you create new realities, new experiences, and even new possibilities now.*

*Now we know that people relax more deeply when you see trees, just the presence of the beautiful wood is a present to the mind in this present moment. So you can present this pleasant presence to yourself for your own pleasure now if you like. And I am wondering if you are imaging high, craggy mountains and evergreens, symbols of enduring life, or if you are imagining a more deciduous forest, where the cycles of life move and flow, one into another. I don't know if you are imaging the young light green and fragrant flowers of an early spring, perhaps rhododendron and mountain laurel, with the promise of a new life. Or maybe you are imagining the fullness of a beautiful summer under a golden sun, brining warmth and life an illumination to your life. Or perhaps the riot of colors of autumn, reds and oranges and yellows that bring so much beauty into your life. Or even the white white beauty of a gorgeous winterscape, where a low, white stark sun brings piercing illumination and clarity to your life, drawing contrasts under a deep blue winter sky.*

*I wonder if you can imagine all that as you are relaxing and breathing deeply now, noticing how the chair supports you, in the same way your powerful creative other-than-conscious supports you now, supporting your heart beating over 86 thousand beats a day, rhythmically, naturally normally.*

*But you can enjoy sitting on that porch, rocking, feeling the day, experiencing the trees and the view and the breeze, knowing that this is your time to pretend or to imagine or even to create; to imagine a new story, a new reality, new possibilities. And, as you think of those leaves, early green flowing the beautiful reds and oranges and yellows, the true reality of change.*

*Now when it is time, when it is absolutely time for you, you rise from the rocker, standing on your own two feet, solid and secure, and you begin to move forward now, walking across the porch, noticing how your body moves easily, fluidly, comfortably. Looking out at nature you naturally only do things that you believe to be productive and beneficial for your life and for your body.*

*As you step up to the door of the cabin or lodge, you know that this is your time to step into a new place. To leave behind the things that are no longer needed or necessary for your life. This is your time to step into a new place.*

*A door is a transition into a new place, almost another reality. It's interesting to know that people forget when they walk through a doorway. We've all walked into another room and wondered exactly why we came in there. In the same way you would walk through a doorway, knowing what was behind you, but simply forgetting about it, just toss it away, throw it away, let it go, and move forward through the door. This is your time to create a change.*

*As you step into the room, you notice that you are stepping into a room with three doors. In this room with three doors you have a deep sense within you that in this room with three doors you are absolutely safe, totally comfortable, completely at peace. You come here to see things through new eyes, from better and healthier perspectives. You come here to realize at any one moment in time there are only an infinity of things you can think and do, a million choices you can make. You come here to realize that you own your emotions. No one else has control over your emotions (unless you give it to them, and you can always take it back). You come here to create.*

*Now, as we begin, I'd like to invite you to think of a situation, a circumstance, an event, even perhaps a conversation—the sort of thing which in the past has been frustrating or difficult or a problem for you. Perhaps this has been a source of stress or anxiety or frustration or depression or even anger.*

*As you think of this difficult or frustrating or problematic event or circumstance or situation or even conversation from the past, the sort of thing that has been a problem for you in the past, I wonder if you can imagine it happening—if you can see it playing out in your mind. Perhaps you can imagine it playing out over there on a* small television screen, the kind of boxy little television that someone might have had perhaps in their kitchen.

And as you see that difficult or problematic event or conversation or whatever that used to be a problem whenever playing on that small screen way over there, you realize you can just take the remote and step away from all that.

As you take that control now, you can press a button, noticing that as you take control, the colors in that old vision from the past are just fading away, fading to shades of gray and black and white, fading away like an old black and white movie, washed out, something from the past.

And as you take that control again, pressing another button, this time you notice the sounds are just fading away, washing out, quieter and quieter. The sounds of that circumstance, whatever it used to be, the sounds of voices (if there were voices). Just fading to peaceful silence, like you just hit a mute button. And you realize it is like you are watching an old black and white silent movie, like something from the ancient past.

And as you firmly take that control now, pressing another button, this time you notice that all the motion in the picture is just fading away, everything slowing down, slower and slower and slower, until it all just freezes in place, like you hit a pause button. And you realize you are not even looking at a movie; you are just looking at a picture, like a photograph, like an old black and white snapshot. Something from the past, something that perhaps used to be, but it has nothing to do with your present, certainly not your future.

As you take that remote and step further away from all that, you can just shut it down, shut it off, take the power from it. Just hit the off button and let it go.

Now, here in the room with three doors you are absolutely safe, totally comfortable, completely at peace. As you consider the first door, you realize that once you step through that door you will be stepping into that same old situation or circumstance, event or even conversation that used to be a problem back in the past.

*You will step into it, experience it, breathe it in, feel it. Be there in that moment.*

*But you notice that you will not react to it the way you used to! No! You notice you respond in a way which is so positive, productive, beneficial that you may surprise even yourself.*

*It doesn't matter right now if you don't know now exactly how you are going to respond now in a way that is so effective and rewarding. There is a part of you, a powerful, problem solving, creative other-than-conscious part of you, which sees connections you don't see consciously. Which sees solutions and possibilities and opportunities. And this powerful creative problem solving part of you will provide you with solutions that are so effective, joyful, even life-affirming that you may surprise even yourself at just how well you respond now.*

*So step up to the first door. Take in a deep breath. Feel your shoulders roll back, your chin roll upward, your confidence soar. When you are ready, when you are absolutely ready, step through the door now.*

*Be there in that moment. Feel it. Breathe it in. Experience it. That old situation or circumstance or situation or even conversation, the sort of thing that has been a problem back in the past is happening one more time.*

*But notice that you are not reacting the way you used to. No! You are responding in a way that is so effective, positive, productive, beneficial, life-affirming, even joyous that you may be surprising even yourself. So take a moment for that to work itself out now. And when my voice returns you will only relax even more deeply now.*

[• Pause 10 seconds]

*Deeper now, drifting, dreaming, floating, flowing, calm, relaxed, completely at peace. The room with three doors. You are absolutely safe, totally comfortable, completely at peace.*

*As you consider the second door,*

[• dismissive tone here:] *you realize that once you step through the second door that same old thing that used to be a problem back in the past is going to be happening one* more time. But you're sure not going to react the way you used to, because that doesn't even make sense any more.

[• firm tone, then your normal relaxing voice:] No! You won't even respond the way you did behind the first door, as wonderful as that was. No, this time your powerful creative other-than-conscious is going to give you a new way to respond that is so rewarding, fulfilling, positive, beneficial that you may surprise even yourself.

So step up to the second door now. Feel your shoulders roll back, your chin roll upward, your confidence soar. When you are ready, when you are absolutely ready, step through the door now. That same old thing that used to be a problem back in the past is happening one more time. But you are sure not reacting the way you used to. No! Notice how you are responding in a way that is so positive, productive, beneficial, life-affirming, even joyful that you may surprise even yourself! So take a moment for that to play out now, and when my voice returns you will only go deeper now.

[• Pause 10 seconds]

Deeper now, drifting dreaming flowing!

The third door. You know once you step through the third door, that same old thing will be happening one more time, but you're sure not reacting the way you used to—no, that doesn't even make sense anymore!

[• smile and begin chuckling or laughing as you speak now:] No! This time you're going to respond in a way that is so ridiculous, something so silly, so funny that you perhaps wouldn't even do it in real life. But you can just imagine it now, and enjoy yourself. So step through the third door now, and just have a good time!

[• Pause 10 seconds (and you are done with the chuckling, so after your voice can return to your normal relaxing voice]

Deeper now, drifting, dreaming, floating, flowing, calm, relaxed, completely at peace. The room with three doors. You are absolutely safe, totally comfortable, completely at peace. You come here to see things through new eyes, from better and healthier perspectives. You come here to realize at any one moment in time there are only an infinity of things you can think and do, a million choices you can *make. You come here to realize that you own your emotions. No one else has control over your emotions. No matter what happens in the world around you, you can be okay. You can come here any time.*

*As you are listening to my voice, if this is a time when you need to be sleeping deeply, relaxing comfortably, then as your head touches the pillow and you pull the sheets or blankets over you, you can begin to drift into even deeper, more healing states of sleep. Knowing that as you sleep your powerful problem solving creative other-than-conscious is always there with you, always taking care of you.*

*And you can dream the dreams of changes you are making, specific steps you are taking to create your life, to create the future you desire. Deep even breaths, deeper now.*

*Of course if this is the time for you to open your eyes now, to make the most of your day, to create your reality and to step moment by moment into your bright, vibrant future, then you can come back into the room now. When you are ready to feel particularly good for no particular reason, when you are ready to see things through new eyes from better and healthier perspectives, then at that moment your eyes will open! You will be wide awake! Wide awake feeling great! And realizing, of course, that every day, in every way, your life is getting better, your world is getting better, and this is so!*

# 3 FADING PHOTOGRAPHS
*metaphors for releasing the past and embracing the future*

I can feel the cold heat of her rage.

We met two minutes earlier, for the first time, in the waiting room. She is in my office now, not yet a client, considering my services.

"It's good if we just have a conversation," I say. "What would you like to ask me or tell me?"

"What I want to tell you is on that paper."

It is a five-page, single-spaced, typewritten document, with plentiful ALL CAPS. The paper is not new, perhaps just a little yellowed. It is her story.

"Please let me take a moment and read it." There is true horror on the pages. Her father silenced her pitiable young teenage protest that she could become pregnant by saying he would wear a rubber. Her mother was not only complicit in the abuse, but added to it herself. I feel queasy.

We look at each other. She is 60 now, Overweight, but in that solid way that portends defensiveness. Her hair is in a short bob that I associate with older Southern women. It fits who she is, but somehow is incongruous with the rage.

"I'm glad you didn't tell me that story in your own voice, and I'm glad this isn't in your handwriting," I begin. "There is power in your own voice and writing—your subconscious believes it—and this is a very destructive story. If we are to be successful, you need to get to the point where you will never tell that story again. Not because you're suppressing it, but because you have dealt with those emotions, and moved past it, and let it go."

She told me she wrote it a few years earlier at the urging of her sister. She is tired of telling it.

"I hate my mother. And my father." The vehemence is fresh on her face, although the perpetrators are long dead. "When I die I want to be cremated and buried between them so I can give them hell for eternity."

"They are still living rent-free in your head," I say. We talk. She has three failed marriages. The most recent divorce becomes final in a month.

"I don't have any relationships. I'm isolated. No one is close."

"I often compare isolation and intimacy to a brick wall, a castle tower around you," I say, pantomiming a mason laying bricks in place, building up the levels. "Usually I talk about how, when the bricks start to come down"—I motion as if bricks are being taken down, level by level, creating an opening in the imaginary wall—"that it is intimacy. It is also vulnerability, because intimacy and vulnerability are the same thing. You become exposed, naked before someone else, open to being loved deeply or hurt bitterly. I talk about how it is not healthy for one person in a relationship to have more bricks down than the other person."

"But there is no point in talking about that with you, is there, because no bricks are down, are they? Anywhere. You have the tower of Babel, built all the way up to the sky." My hands indicate an invisible castle tower, a column of cold stone soaring up through the ceiling.

"No," she says. "It's hard."

I can see the pain on her face. "It's hard being Rapunzel, trapped in your own tower."

She nods. "I have passed my hate on to my children." I can see the tears beginning to well up in her eyes. "I can't take it anymore. Something has to change. I feel like I'm lost in the woods."

"More like a haunted forest," I say. "Aren't you tired of the trees throwing apples at you like in *The Wizard of Oz?*"

She looks at me. The pattern interrupt is working, and her reality is shaking a bit.

"I'm a wilderness guide," I say. "I've been through a lot of dark forests. I have the skills for it—I can start a fire in the rain, and pitch a tent. I've been through a lot of wildernesses, my own and other people's. But I have never been through *your* forest before, and I don't know what we'll encounter. I don't know the path through. But I know I can be with you and help you, and together we will find a path through the wilderness. It will have to be your path, because it is your forest."

She nods. "You're not like other therapists, are you." The way she says it, it is not really a question. "I've been to a lot of therapists, and none of them has helped. You don't seem like them. You're not saying the same things at all."

"Thank you," I answer. "Is that the only copy of that story?" I ask, and she says it is. "Good. Can I keep it? Because you need to get rid of it now."

She nods. Her face is a little more open now. It's just barely showing, but I believe I can see hope.

I begin to walk through a terrible dark forest with Rapunzel, knowing monsters haunt this place, that a frightened girl is walking beside me, but I am not afraid. We will find her path. I am a wilderness guide.

## Focus on what you want

It is probably safe to think of psychotherapy as falling into two distinct groups: problem-focused therapies and solution-focused therapies

Freudian psychoanalysis exemplified a problem-focused therapy. The key idea was to explore the past in order to gain insight into what went wrong. Once the client has insight, then somehow the problem should be magically fixed. Except, of course, that gaining insight into the past or even into supposed causes does not necessarily change any of the current experience of the problem, and the magic fix often fails to happen.

As noted in the first chapter, the complexity of life, retroactively-ascribed causes and false memory can quickly turn the search for causes into a dark path.

There is the additional problem that you get what you focus on. It is important to focus on what you want, not on what you don't want.

Solution-focused therapies are different. The basic questions are, Where are you now? Where do you want to be? How do we get from here to there? De Shazer's miracle question, discussed in the first chapter, exemplifies a solution-focused approach. Another Solution-Focused Brief Therapy (SFBT) technique, focusing on exceptions, also exemplifies this approach. The goal is to look for areas where the client experienced some degree of success, and then to seek ways to create more of that.

A solution focus is not about ignoring the past. The problem is that past emotions can intrude into the present and wreak havoc in the now. As we noted in Chapter 2, something happens and triggers a reaction based on past experience.

It's critical to realize that these emotions do not belong here in the present. Think of it this way: You have more wisdom, life experience and emotional strength now than you did in the past. At some point in the past a younger you experienced a problem, or even a trauma, and that younger you did the best he or she could to handle things with the resources available then. At that time an emotion was created that was associated with that type of event or circumstance.

Fast forward to the present. Something happens that is similar to that past event or circumstance, and that old emotion from the past, that learned response, kicks in. You react. But that emotion does not belong here in the present. It is a relic of the past, of an earlier time when you had less, perhaps much less, wisdom, life experience and emotional strength, and fewer–perhaps far fewer–resources.

In essence, this is importing the emotions of the past into the present—where they don't belong—and it may even be projecting them into the future.

**Guilt and worry**

Guilt is one example of importing emotions from the past into the present in an unhealthy way. Obviously, if there is a way to make amends in the present for wronging someone in the past, that should be done, as long as this does not cause further harm in the present. Those are the eighth and ninth steps of a twelve-step program: 8. Make a list of all persons we had harmed, and became willing to make amends to them all. 9. Make direct amends to such people wherever possible, except when to do so would injure them or others.

One purpose of making amends is to release guilt, so if this is possible, clients should do it. If not, guilt is a wasted emotion, and it needs to be released.

Worry is the mirror image of guilt. Where guilt is importing problems from the past into the present, worry is emotionally projecting potential problems into the future. We are the stories we tell ourselves. We emphasize certain things in our lives and deemphasize others. If you change the emphases, you change your life. The point of narrative therapy and motivational interviewing—like SFBT, other solution focused approaches to psychotherapy—is to rework personal meaning at a deep, emotional and existential level. Guilt usually has some grounding in actual events. Worry is just anticipation of something that never has been, and may never be (although people can create the problem through self-fulfilling prophecy, but that's a very bad idea).

Worry is using the imagination to create a future you don't want—to pre-catastrophize the future. Remember, the Ericksonian unconscious is about seeking health and healing. Your clients need to use their powerful imagination to create a future they *do* want.

It is impossible to worry and take action at the same time. We just don't have the emotional energy to do it. As we will consider in Chapter 5, it is critical to realize that individuals can take meaningful action to determine what life will be like. One solution to worry is to actually evaluate the problem. Fear hides in the dark and makes scary noises at night. The solution is to turn on the light and actually look at it. Then you can plan to deal with it.

Incidentally, motivational studies show that while imagining future success is nice, it is imagining the actual, specific, concrete steps to achieve that success that build motivation and drive to accomplish goals. As you help your clients consider those specific steps, it may help to remember that goals need to be SMarT: **S**pecific, **M**easurable, and **T**ime-sensitive. As your clients think of what they will do to create the future they want, encourage them to be specific, to know how they will tell when they have achieved the goal, and give themselves a deadline. Pro tip: Setting a deadline is essential.

### Forgiveness

Forgiveness can also come into play. I tell my clients that, at one level, forgiveness is releasing negative emotion toward someone else (an abuser or offender), even though that person has seriously wronged you. Holding onto the negative emotion continues to give the offender emotional power over you (even if that person is no longer actively in your life, or even if that person is dead). An Internet meme states that unforgiveness is like drinking poison and expecting it to harm someone else. It's true; the negative emotion churns inside, even if the person is gone. Failing to forgive simply allows someone who has seriously hurt you to continue to live rent-free in your head.

The main therapeutic arguments against forgiveness come from therapists who work with victims of emotional, physical or sexual abuse or with those who are recovering from substance abuse. It is critical to realize that forgiveness is not reconciliation. The offender or abuser has forfeited the right to a relationship, and reestablishing that relationship may be very dangerous.

As we will consider in Chapter 6, the nature of abuse is to destroy the victim's sense of being able to take meaningful action to determine what her or his life will be like. Abuse creates emotional dependence on the abuser. Under no circumstances should this be permitted to continue. Forgiveness in an abuse context is not about getting back together. It is about ridding life of the abuser, emotionally as well as physically.

Sometimes clients may also need to forgive themselves. This is usually about letting go of guilt from the past that's based on the destructive narratives and expectations of others. In terms of cognitive behavioral therapy (CBT), it is about getting rid of irrational shoulds and musts; that is, ridding the self of the emotional need to live by someone else's standards or expectations.

It is also possible that your client needs to forgive him or herself for something they did that truly caused harm, as we discussed a few pages back regarding guilt.

I remember Dave walking into my office for the first time. He was distraught because so many things were spinning out of control. At work, he was having trouble making people do what he wanted. And now his relationship with his wife had exploded. She had left.

As he continued to talk, I had a growing sense of horror. It became clear that I was listening to the abuser in an abusive relationship. Dave had emotionally (and, I later discovered, physically) abused her. Somehow she had developed the strength to stand up for herself and leave.

This was rare, because abusers don't usually seek help. I saw this as a golden opportunity: If I could help Dave become more healthy, that would save any number of people in the future from being harmed by him. I needed to help him reframe the emotions driving the abuse.

The desire to control other people is the essence of abuse. Conditional love, guilt manipulation, bullying, objectification, physical and sexual abuse flow from that. If you're reading this and you recognize in yourself that need to control others, please find a therapist and work that through. You will help yourself and many, many others. Self-forgiveness is not enough; change needs to happen. Do not try to reestablish relationships with those you have abused; just let them go. It is time to start fresh, in a healthy way.

If your client needs to forgive the self, though—whether it is about things done to them, or things they have done to others, or even some mixture of the two—that's a good idea. Release the negative emotions.

**Fade the past, move forward**

Fading Photographs is not about the past, and it is not problem-focused. The metaphor is used to release problem emotions from the past that are intruding into the present so your client can use that emotional energy to move forward. This process is about solutions, about becoming untangled from the past so you can create the life desired. Release the past; it is gone. Just let it go. Enjoy the process!

One additional note: This sort of process is excellent for addressing problems from the past. To address serious trauma, a regression is probably more appropriate. Serious trauma should be addressed by a licensed therapist or qualified mental health professional, not simply by a lay hypnotist.

ഹ൞ൕൠ

## The Fading Photographs hypnosis process

*As you are relaxing and breathing deeply, you may notice the wonderful sensations of peace moving through your body. The deep rhythm of your heartbeat, the growing heaviness of your eyelids.*

*With your eyes comfortably closed, just let your mind drift where it will. You are aware of everything, yet not aware. You are listening with your subconscious mind while your conscious mind is far away and not listening. Your conscious mind is far away and not listening. Your subconscious mind is listening and hearing everything while your conscious mind drifts and flows. Your conscious mind does not mind while your subconscious mind minds everything for you.*

*You can remember everything with your subconscious mind, but you cannot remember everything with your conscious mind. While your conscious mind sleeps and lets go, you feel fine as your subconscious mind mines for fine gold, or finds just what is fine for you.*

*Remembering what you need to remember and forgetting what you can forget. It does not matter if you forget. Your powerful memory serves you well, and your subconscious mind dips into that well and finds just what you need to find, whatever is gold for you to reach your goals.*

*Reaching your goals you can let go. You need not remember what you can forget. Remembering to forget by forgetting to remember, your subconscious remembers everything that is helpful for you, so you can let your subconscious listen and remember while your conscious sleeps and forgets.*

*With your eyes comfortably closed listen with your subconscious mind, and when you're listening very very carefully, your conscious mind will not mind what it lets go while your subconscious mind flows. You know your subconscious mind knows just what you need to know, so your conscious mind can sleep and flow.*

*You know you know that time when you felt really good about yourself for something you've said or done or not done; or it may be a compliment someone paid you that triggered those wonderful feelings.*

*Let your subconscious mind provide you now with a memory of a time when you felt really good about yourself. Perhaps you accomplished something you were proud of, or maybe you were being complimented for your effort. The content of the memory is not the goal right now, what's important now is the feeling this memory created within you.*

*When you have that memory, step into it and breathe it in. Breathe the way you were breathing at the time. Feel the colors, the vibrancy of this wonderful memory. See the situation you are in, and who is with you. What you are doing. Where you are. Fill in the details—the time of year, spring, summer, autumn, winter; the time of day—morning, afternoon or evening. What you are wearing and feeling*

38

and seeing and touching, if anything. Hear what is being said here, if anything is said; or any other sounds, or fragrances.

And really let yourself experience how it felt inside. Those good, positive, strong feelings. Confident and self assured feelings. Feel them in your body!

And you can allow those feelings to grow stronger and more positive while you breathe in a really long, full breath through your nose, and press together the thumb and finger of your right hand. Feel your shoulders roll back, your chin roll upward, your confidence soar!

Because in the future, whenever you breathe in that long deep breath through your nose and press together the thumb and finger of the right hand, you will feel those good, strong, confident feelings filling your being. You can feel these good, strong, confident feelings any time you like, in any situation. These good, strong, confident feelings are becoming more and more a part of you, and you are becoming that stronger, more confident person.

And remember, any time you want to feel even more confident, breathe in that long deep breath through your nose and press together the thumb and finger of the right hand, and you will feel these good strong confident feelings filling your being. You can feel wonderful, calmer, more relaxed, much more confident than ever before. And you know what it is like to feel these good strong confident feelings. You can remember and re-experience these feelings that are becoming more and more a permanent part of you.

So go ahead now and take in a deep, deep breath, letting that breath flow, and giving yourself permission to journey back through time. To remember to forget things that aren't worth remembering by forgetting to remember them. Remembering what you need to remember and forgetting what you can forget; remembering only things that are positive, life-giving, even forgiving for you as you move forward. Organizing your powerful memory so you will possess a memory that will serve you well for the rest of your life.

So feel the deep relaxation flowing through your body as you give yourself permission to journey back through *time. Back, perhaps, to elementary school memories or perhaps even further. Some people can remember back as early as age three, while most adults have trouble remembering much of what happened before age 10, and most children start losing earlier memories by age seven. And while very young children may not have the brain structures or language for rational memory, there is an emotional part of you that may somehow experience feelings back to birth. None of that is important right now. What's important is that you are giving yourself permission to journey back to the earliest memory you choose to remember today, so that you can move forward and organize memories that are useful and no longer useful for you and for your life experience.*

*There is a part of you that knows the past only provides two valid things: happy memories and lessons learned. Any moment you spend on the past that is not a happy memory or lesson learned is simply importing yesterday's problems into today, where they don't belong or even have a place.*

*You will take the negative times and place them in the large picture frames behind you, allowing these photographs to fade to black and white images, fading away like old snapshots from the past. Fading away like forgotten photographs hanging on a wall, washed out by the bright sunlight of other days. As these memories fade away, part of you gains a lesson learned, so you can simply allow that old memory from the past to fade away, like an old photograph bleached out by the rays of the bright shining sun. Now I don't know if this is the golden warmth of a summer sun, or the cold pure white of a low winter sun. Just let it go. Seasons shift. Feel the change.*

*Destructive voices of the past are like the cracking static of a radio from yesteryear. You simply take the remote control, step back, turn them down, tune them out, turn them off.*

*You will find as you release these memories your mind will be filled with such optimism and joy. As you let go of the entanglements of the past it is so much easier to see clearly in the present, and to take specific steps today to create your future. Naturally you are spending your time*

40

*doing things that are productive, positive, life-affirming. So take the time to remember to forget by forgetting to remember.*

*As you encounter wonderful, positive, joyous memories, memories you can enjoy remembering, step into them. Think of one of the most beautiful times you can recall now. It could be a glorious morning, a perfect afternoon, a quiet evening. Some time with friends or family members— or even some time on your own. Some time in your life that is beautiful.*

*As you have that beautiful memory, step into it, breathe it in. Breathe the way you were breathing at the time, allowing the colors of this space to become bright and beautiful, the sounds to become clear and vibrant; feel the way your body feels, positive, joyful. You are becoming comfortable with the idea of feeling comfortable, of feeling good for no particular reason at all. You truly deserve it.*

*Allow the good, positive, warm, life-affirming memories to flow. They become as natural to you to remember as your breathing, as normal a part of your life as your heartbeat.*

*You are learning to release the past. Remembering that unforgiveness is like drinking poison and expecting it to harm someone else, you are learning to forgive. You are learning to forget. You are moving on. Forgiving, forgetting, and moving on, even when it means leaving negative people from your past out of your life. You are moving forward. You are becoming comfortable with the idea of feeling good, thinking positive thoughts. You truly deserve it. There is so much more joy ahead of you, so much more love and harmony for you to enjoy.*

*So now that you've learned to remember to forget by forgetting to remember, to forgive and forget and move on, to let go of negative, less-than-positive memories, imagine that you are throwing that old photograph out, so that you know that it happened, but you no longer need to remember it.*

*It's interesting to know that people forget when they walk through a doorway. We've all walked into another room and wondered exactly why we came in there. In the same way you would walk through a doorway, knowing what was behind you, but simply forgetting about it, just toss it away, throw it away, let it go, and close the door.*

*Notice now the relaxation as it moves through your body, clearing your mind and allowing your body to melt. This moment we call now is the most powerful moment in time. Now you are alive, now you are taking specific steps to bring joy into your life. Taking action and accomplishing goals is becoming second nature to you—imagine that!*

*Now is the most beautiful moment in time. Now is the time you are taking the time to create all the physical, mental and emotional changes you desire, to create the life you desire living now, filled with joy, expectancy, and even opportunity. Now you are taking meaningful action that will determine what your life will be like now and in the future. The seconds are like hours here, so take the time now to imagine the specific steps you are taking now that will create the future you desire.*

*So now as you journey back through time to the very earliest memory you find now, allow yourself to move forward from that moment to this moment in time, sitting here, listening to my voice. As you move from the past to the present your powerful powerful mind sorts and categorizes all the memories that come up. Some you breathe in, others you simply allow to fade away. You are gaining lessons learned and happy memories.*

*As happy memories come, step into them, breathe them in, experience them in bright living color, filled with energy, life, vitality.*

*Any negative times that arise—step away from them, putting a picture frame around them. Make the frame old like you might find at a garage sale, and dusty— something representing the ancient past—something you could care less about; something that no longer has a place in your life. And as you place it behind you, feel yourself simply forgiving the situation. Whether it is your father or mother, another family member, a romantic partner, a friend, colleague, or even an acquaintance—whoever it is, forgive them for not living up to what you wanted them to be, and just let that go.*

*Imagine that person is forgiving you, perhaps, for not living up to what they wanted you to be, and as you* release and you allow and you let that go now feel the healing flow through your body, your mind, your emotions. For as you forgive and let that go you can release the enormous power you've wasted, bound up in the past, releasing that enormous power to flow positively into the present. Using that enormous power to create such love, such joy with those in your life today. Experiencing the wonderful feeling of love, forgiveness, and freedom in your life now.

Remembering to forget by forgetting to remember it is easy to remember the positive, beautiful times, to create joy today, to create the life you desire today.

Even now your mind is traveling forward into your future, creating powerful positive possibilities, creating goals and priorities, creating a path forward; remembering that you are far greater than you thought you were, far greater than you thought you could be, you are dreaming big, positive, beautiful dreams, as your powerful subconscious mind, without you even realizing it, is creating specific plans; the action steps to move forward.

There is a part of you that realizes that worry is simply using your imagination to create a future you don't want— and you simply do not have the time, the space, or the place for that. Realizing that it is almost impossible to worry and plan or take action at the same time, you are using your powerful creative imagination to create the future you do want.

Even now you can imagine your future, bright and beautiful, a vivid gorgeous painting. Even now you can imagine specific changes you are making that will create the life you desire to live. Even now you are realizing you are worth the time, the effort, the energy of change. Even now you are loving and taking time for yourself. You are worth the time, the effort, the energy of change.

Even now you are thinking about reworking the past, taking action in the present, and focusing your life on the future, focusing on the specific steps you will take now to create your life, to be all you can be. Even now you realize you are learning new ways to manage memories, new ways to live life. Even now you are beginning to dream beautiful dreams.

*If this is a time for you to sleep and dream—dreaming of changes made to even your earliest memories, where you will hear beautiful words about yourself, about how you were wanted, desired, expected; the inner message will be so positive you will focus forward on the positive and simply release the negative upon awakening.*

*Of course if this is a time for you to be awake, embracing the day, and moving forward with your life, then at that moment your eyes will open. When you are ready to remember to forget the emotional baggage of the past like a dream fading as you awaken; when you are ready to see through new eyes from better and healthier perspectives, when you are ready to create your future, then your eyes will open, you will be wide awake, feeling renewed, feeling positive, and remembering that every day, in every way, your life is getting better, your world is getting better, and this is so!*

# 4 SLEEP!
*suggestion for falling and staying asleep*

It is 3 a.m.-ish. I'm in bed, awake, perhaps. This book is mostly written. I look at this unusual bit of dreamy wakefulness as an opportunity, and allow myself to flow to the metaphors: The Three Doors, The Surfer. My mind dreams and wanders. I recall a young client in pain from a skim board accident that happened on a beautiful day at the beach; Captain Picard's adventures in an asteroid field; two clients who were laid off; a tragic quote from Hamlet, who as prince of Denmark should have been able to take care of himself. I trust my unconscious to create the images I need, trust my unconscious to let me know in the morning, and I sleep.

I awaken, an hour later than I normally would (thank you, unconscious me, for giving me back that time to be refreshed), with the morning blocked off to write. The words flow for a good while, and then the real world interrupts: I deal with some client scheduling issues, and the office voicemail service that isn't working properly. I'm writing at home, so now is a good time to take a nice, long, hot shower.

My creative self opens up again as my mind skips from a long-past conversation in a dress shop in San Diego to Stevie Nicks singing about an Irish enchantress, dreams and love. When I return to writing, it's a gentle task, fueled by my unconscious. It's okay to sleep, perchance to dream; sleep is a gift, and lucid dreaming is revelry. Creativity is an unconscious process, gentle, and it flows best unencumbered by the rational mind.

## Sleep is a serious issue

The U.S Centers for Disease Control and Prevention (CDC) calls sleeplessness an epidemic, associated with industrial, auto and medical accidents, as well as high blood pressure, depression, diabetes, obesity and cancer. Other research indicates that sleep deficits are strongly associated with attention deficit hyperactivity disorder (ADHD), and may well be the real issue in addressing problems of focus (Thakkar, 2013). Since 1995 the National Institutes of Health (NIH) have strongly recommended hypnosis to treat insomnia.

While the Three Doors and Fading Photographs are generally great places to start with clients suffering from anxiety or stress, Beautiful Deep Sleep is a great third session choice (or even a second or first session choice). Lack of sleep diminishes a person's ability to handle stress and generally makes everything worse, so getting healthy sleep in place is critical. Sleeplessness can also be a vicious cycle; lack of sleep makes it more difficult to handle stress, which disturbs sleep, which makes stress worse, and on and on and on.

Of course, if the issue is insomnia, it makes sense to start here, perhaps with The Three Doors as a follow up. Many times therapists consider whether the issue with insomnia is trouble initially falling asleep, or difficulty returning to sleep if awakened during the night. This process is designed to address both issues.

## The bedroom

Studies show that people sleep better in an uncluttered environment. I tell my clients that it's important to create a bedroom that's a place where they can go to relax. Everyone truly deserves a good night's sleep. So take the time to create a space set aside for that purpose. Clean up the clutter. Create a welcoming, relaxed space; it does not need to look like the cover of

*House Beautiful* or some showplace from HGTV, but it should be peaceful.

Start with a relaxing color. The client decides what is relaxing, of course, but probably it will be some light shade of blue, green, amethyst or beige, and probably not something like red, orange or bright yellow.

The bedroom is for only two things, and neither of these involves electronic devices. Get the television out of the bedroom. We will discuss sleep cycles in a few pages, but suffice it to say here television technology involves a flicker—consciously imperceptible, but it definitely moves people toward a more awake state.

I tell clients to turn the alarm clock so that it faces away from them as they sleep. It is normal to sleep more deeply *and* more lightly; generally people are not aware of these cycles, and simply feel as though they have slept through the night. But if you cycle to a light state and become aware of a red 3:34 a.m. in your face, that may register and make you feel as if you've been lying awake all night. Those clocks that project the time onto the ceiling should be thrown away. On the other hand, a clock that awakens by gently increasing illumination in the room is a good idea. If a client has real trouble waking, there are smartphone apps with alarms that won't turn off until you stand and turn while holding the phone in your hands. But once sleep improves, waking up should not be a problem.

By the way, our other-than-conscious does not like the alarm any more than we do, so as sleep improves we often find that we naturally awaken a minute or two before the alarm goes off. That offers a moment to get up, stretch and turn off the alarm before it blares. I also tell my clients that if the alarm goes off, get up. Hitting the snooze button will allow you to drift back down just enough to feel really worn out when the snooze alarm jolts you back awake. Most people feel more refreshed if they forget the clock even has a snooze button.

I recommend against charging devices in the bedroom, but at least cover the charge lights. A night light is fine, but it should be a low gentle light, not a red or green LED violating the darkness.

White noise machines are relatively inexpensive and can be very helpful. These range from machines that simply make sound like a fan (without the breeze) to more involved machines that play everything from nature sounds (a babbling brook or gentle tide) to music. Some companies market dreamy music designed to carry the user down into the cycle of sleep. This won't be rock or rap, and it won't have lyrics; think baroque or light jazz. A beautiful, relaxing tabletop fountain is another white noise option to consider.

Many people feel is if they have the best ideas as they are falling asleep; we'll talk about relaxation and creativity later. A client who lies awake with the mind racing should probably keep paper and a pen or a voice recorder by the bed to capture thoughts, and then give themselves permission to relax and sleep. There is no need to lie awake trying to hold onto an idea when one can simply record a note. In the morning your client will either find gibberish or a fantastic idea. Either way, there is never any sense to losing sleep over it.

**Time for sleep**

We have all had the experience of walking through a door into a room, and then forgetting why we entered. You can help your client turn this to his or her advantage. Each of is us is valuable, and the last 10 or 20 minutes of the day (or even a half hour) is the time for self care. Encourage your client to take time earlier in the evening to leave everything they need for the morning in its place, so they know they will be unrushed in the morning. Of course, it is also a good idea to advise them to avoid stimulants like caffeine or nicotine in the evening. When it is 20 minutes or so before bedtime, this is the time to lay aside all the cares and concerns of the day. This is the time to turn off the television or computer or other devices, and leave them in the living room. As they walk through the door of their bedroom, they should give themselves the pleasure of thinking of this as their time to rejuvenate.

Take time for evening hygiene; this is the time to pamper (even men). Brush teeth, get changed for bed.

Enjoy an intimate interlude. When it is time to sleep, the client has mentally prepared the self for sleep. They are ready.

**Cycles and sleep subjectivity**

People tend to think of sleep as an on/off switch, but it's not. Awareness and relaxation are a continuum, and the movement from wakefulness to sleep and back is like a dimmer switch. This is a physical phenomena, not just subjective experience; we are talking brain wave cycles; what an electroencephalograph (EEG) measures.

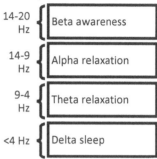

When you are fully alert, your brain waves cycle at up to 20 cycles per second, or Hertz (Hz). That upper level is called Beta awareness. Have you ever had a time when you were just relaxed, doing something you really enjoy, losing track of time? Or perhaps you had a great idea while you were enjoying a nice, warm shower? That is Alpha relaxation, which is a brain wave cycle of 14 to nine Hz.

If you've ever had a moment, relaxing on the sofa, drifting in and out while the television plays in the background or the book gently slips from your hand, when someone would think you were asleep, but you know you really are not sleeping, that is Theta relaxation, nine to four Hz. Hypnosis takes place in Theta; the frontal lobe of the brain (the seat of cognitive processing) is gently slowing down, and the limbic system (the emotional you) is becoming more prominent, so this is a great state to facilitate emotional change.

Deep Delta sleep is four Hz or less, down to about one-and-a-half Hz (brain death is no cycle, so that is pretty objective). Through the night you continue to cycle more deeply and more lightly, sometimes up into Theta or possibly even a low Alpha state. A normal adult sleep cycle is about 90 minutes. Early in the evening, the last 20 minutes of the cycle may be rapid eye movement

(REM) sleep, where you dream. By the end of the night, perhaps the last 90 minutes may be REM sleep.

You need less sleep as you move through the lifespan. Eight hours of sleep a night is an optimal average for a mid-life adult. A client in his late 80s came to me complaining that he was not sleeping more than six hours a night.

"How do you feel in the morning?" I asked. "Do you feel good?"

"Well, I am 88." he smiled. "Other than that I guess I feel fine. I just feel like I should sleep more."

"Congratulations," I replied. "You just get to enjoy more waking time. As long as you're rested and waking naturally, things are fine."

On the other hand, a child, adolescent or even young adult may need more than eight hours of sleep each night. Whatever the age, to find the optimal amount of sleep, you should encourage the client to pay attention to how long they sleep during a long vacation or break. For the first few days they may be making up a sleep deficit. But once they've had four or five nights of going to bed when they want and waking naturally, encourage them to take note of how many hours they sleep. That will be the optimal number of hours for them.

The entire idea of an eight-hour block of sleep at night seems to be an Industrial Age innovation. In pre-industrial Europe people often had sleep and "second sleep." The high latitudes of Europe create very long nights in winter, and in the days before electricity, people would often retire with the sun. Then they would get up in the middle of the night, perhaps to do chores, eat, have sex, or even visit with neighbors. This would be followed by a "second sleep" prior to sunrise. The total hours slept is the key, not the eight-hour block.

While the other processes in this book are all designed to change waking state behaviors, hypnosis is an even better fit for addressing sleep behaviors. After all, it is hard to understand what "trying to go to sleep" actually means. "Trying" is a waking state, Beta awareness effort, while sleep is Delta at the other end of the scale. To "try to sleep" is a Zen kōan, like trying to think of the sound of one hand clapping. It does not actually make sense. Furthermore, in terms of hypnosis—and therefore emotion—"try" is the language of failure. A stage hypnotist may pose someone in a position, taking advantage of the natural catalepsy or paralysis that accompanies sleep, and then tell them to "try to move but you cannot;" the person cannot move.

Lucid dreaming, or the awareness that you are dreaming as it is happening so that you can turn the dream story in directions you want, is associated with REM, and typically happens just before waking. If your client has sleep issues and realizes they are dreaming, you can direct them to just turn the story to allow themselves to move into a relaxing space. In the same way, when an individual becomes aware of a bad dream or even a nightmare, he or she can simply carry the story in a different, more positive direction.

If your client wants to know their dreams or cultivate lucid dreaming, advise them to just roll over and jot them down on that paper they're keeping beside the bed; otherwise, dreams will fade away with the morning light.

Subjectivity is an unreliable way to gauge sleep. I recall Karen, a weight loss client I'd worked with for some time. She told me she felt she'd never been hypnotized.

Now this surprised me, because while most people lose muscle tension in their face when they go under, or their breathing becomes deeper, Karen sort of flopped and sprawled all over the chair and then lay motionless, clearly in a very deep hypnotic state.

"Are you noticing behavior changes?" I asked.

"Sure," she replied. "I'm eating better and less, and I'm much happier about exercising."

"You've lost how much since we started?"

"Two dress sizes!" She beamed.

"So, would it be okay if I continue to not hypnotize you if you continue to succeed?" I asked.

Clearly Karen was under, and the emotional changes were happening, whatever her subjective experience.

Another client, Patricia, during an interactive process where I had her speaking to me while in hypnosis, kept insisting that she was not relaxed enough. I asked her just to pretend and go with it. At one point in the process, she was dealing with a negative emotion that she said she felt in her head and face. I invited her to imagine her hands coming up to her face, and gently pulling that negative emotion away from her face, as if she were pulling away a web or veil. Her hands came up and she began gently miming the physical effort to pull the shroud away. Afterward she told me that she was much deeper than she thought, because her hands were just moving on their own, without her control.

While many clients experience time as passing very quickly in hypnosis—for example, mistaking a 20-minute session (as shown on the recording timer) for five minutes, although occasionally time distortion goes the other way. I once emerged a client who asked me if it was still Tuesday! I assured her that yes, it was; the process took only 22 minutes, and I had not kept her overnight.

Subjective experience is not a reliable guide to time and depth in relaxed states. You may be sleeping more deeply and longer than you think.

## Sleep eating, sleep walking and night terrors

Another nocturnal behavior is sleep eating.

"I think I'm getting up at night and eating," my client said.

"Why do you think that?" I asked.

"In the morning I find cereal boxes out on the counter in the kitchen, and a bowl and spoon in the sink. But I don't remember any of it. Am I okay?"

"Sure, and I can help you with that."

Like sleep walking, sleep eating involves cycling to a light enough state to be up and moving, but not consciously engaged. Simply incorporating suggestions into the sleep process to the effect that, *You are sleeping deeply through the night, finding that it is easy to remember to forget about eating during the night by simply forgetting to remember it. This is your time to rest and sleep. You might get up to go to the bathroom, but other than that you are simply comfortable, staying in bed through the night as long as everything is safe.* This sort of suggestion would naturally fit in the part of the process that deals with being roused at night.

Sleep walking can be addressed in a similar manner. Incidentally, clients who exhibit this type of sleep behavior (somnambulists) are absolutely the best candidates for hypnosis, so this is often very simple to correct.

The ears continue to work during sleep; sounds vibrate the eardrums, the signal is transmitted to the brain and the amygdala handles sensory input, even when the cerebral cortex is fast asleep.

Have you ever had this experience?

(You, waking up suddenly): "I heard something!"

(Groggy partner, roused): "Huh? What? What did you hear?"

(You): "I don't know, but I heard something!"

You heard something because the amygdala registered it—and in this case, registered it as something needing attention. You don't know what you heard, because the part of you that identifies, the cerebral cortex, was fast asleep. So the amygdala roused the cerebral cortex, telling you it's time to get yourself in gear, because something is happening. The amygdala and the rest of the limbic system are all about your survival. It's one reason why we live at the top of the food chain. So you can let yourself sleep because your subconscious will know when you need to awaken.

A word about naps: Daytime napping should allow at least 10 to 20 minutes for an energy boost, or an hour for deeper slow-wave sleep (although you may wake up a bit groggy). An hour and a half provides a full sleep cycle, so that is great, but avoid half-hour naps unless you want to feel groggy for another half hour or so. Most of the time it is a good idea to save your sleep time for the night.

One of the characteristics of Alpha relaxation is losing track of time. The ability to track time is a frontal lobe phenomenon; as the frontal lobe winds down, we lose the ability to keep track of time. This is more pronounced as we drift into Theta or Delta, which are states people perceive as sleep. Your client may feel he or she has tossed and turned or lay awake all night, when in fact it was simply a lighter state of sleep for just a few moments. Give your clients permission to just let that memory or awareness go.

Timelessness is one of two key factors in night terrors. Immortalized by Henry Fuseli's 1781 painting *The Nightmare*, a night terror is the perception that you are trapped and can't move, with a weight or perhaps even a demon on your chest. Night terrors definitely illicit a panic response.

The other key factor in night terrors is the inability to move. Catalepsy or temporary paralysis is a normal part of sleep. We really don't move much while sleeping (although some people experience small hypnic jerks while relaxing – this is actually a sign of relaxing more deeply); if you think about it, thrashing around while sleeping is a good way to get eaten out in nature..

You may recall a time when you've awakened suddenly you couldn't quite move. This only lasts for a second or so, but the loss of time may make it subjectively feel like quite a while. The amygdala kicks in with fast arousal, which feels like a panic response, and, voilà, the perception of night terror.

**Creativity and sleep (Pro tip: it's productive time)**

Another characteristic of Alpha relaxation is creativity. If you think about it, creativity is not a conscious, waking state or logical phenomenon. Creativity happens when the Ericksonian unconscious, that problem-solving part of you that sees connections you didn't see consciously, perceives a possibility, and eureka! there is that epiphany moment of creativity. It's interesting that the original eureka! moment is attributed to Archimedes of Syracuse, for a flash of insight he had while taking a bath. I recall a commercial from a few years back featuring business people in suits all in a large shower, because that's where the leader said he had his best ideas. Often people will say they want to "sleep on it" to consider an idea. Stepping away, taking a break, and breathing deeply are great ways to spur creativity.

Those who are truly stressed and busy should think of sleep time as some of the most valuable time in the 24-

hour day. This is the chance for the creative unconscious to become unleashed, and to gain some of the best ideas. They simply appear with the morning. Be ready. It will be a great day!

## To deepen or emerge?

It is traditional to emerge someone at the end of a hypnosis process; that is, to bring them back into the room. You will notice with this process that I specifically do an emerging, but then continue immediately into a deepener, taking the client into an even deeper state of relaxation. This is because the recording of the process can be used to glide from the Theta hypnotic state straight into relaxed, deeper Delta sleep. If the client is not listening at bedtime and needs to awaken, the emerging should get that done. If it is bed time, raising the client up with the emerging and then dropping him or her with the deepener will cause fractionation, the process in hypnosis where you take someone up then down in order to create a deeper, more relaxed state. This makes the process useful for any time of day.

ഇൽഡൃശൿ

## Beautiful Deep Sleep
## hypnosis process

*With your eyes comfortably closed, just let your mind drift where it will, enjoying deep full breaths. Just breathing in fully, and gently letting go. Allowing your breathing to become very comfortable and rhythmic, very natural and spontaneous.*

*And already beginning to notice the gentle feelings of relaxation moving through your body, which is good for deep hypnosis. Now I don't know whether your feet feel so heavy it is as though they are melting. Or perhaps your hands feel very light, or very heavy, or there may be the gentle pulse of relaxation in the tips of your fingers. Or perhaps your eyelids are so so very heavy that they simply will not open. Whatever you feel, it is appropriate for you. Your powerful subconscious mind knows just what is best for you, now.*

*I'd like to invite you to notice your feet, your feet that feel so so heavy, the toes melting into the soles of the foot, melting into the heel, so relaxed and so comfortable now. You can feel the relaxation flowing across the ankle. You are learning to have faith, and let go. You are learning to get rid of 'shoulds' and 'musts.'*

*As the relaxation flows from the ankle to the knees, notice that the muscles of the shins and calves are melting and flowing, so comfortable. The muscles of the calves melting away, the muscles of the shins flowing away, like warm wax melting, so very comfortable. You are learning to trust yourself and your own instincts. You are listening to that calm, still, always peaceful voice inside.*

*And you can feel the relaxation beginning to flow across the knees toward the hips, as the large muscles of the thighs simply release and let go, so comfortable. Like rubber bands just spilled out, flopping on the table. You are learning that fear and excitement are two sides of the same coin. You are realizing that you are not defined by how much you make or how you earn it.*

*And I wonder if you would like to double the relaxation in your neck and shoulders now, or if you would rather try to keep that stress a little longer while other parts of the body relax first. Never mind, it is not important. You happiness does not depend upon others. So much more important to notice the comfortable relaxation flowing across your hips; the muscles of the bottom releasing, the inner organs of the abdomen moving in their rhythmic, natural functions, as the lower back releases, vertebrae by vertebrae. You realize that you can take meaningful action that will determine what your life will be like. You can feel the muscles of the stomach, the abdomen relaxing.*

*Your breathing is so deep. With each breath in, the muscles of the diaphragm contract, and as those muscles release now, you naturally breathe out, letting go, relaxing. The body naturally relaxing. You are beginning to discover and like yourself. You are experiencing life in a new way, through different eyes, from better and healthier perspectives.*

*So I would like to invite you to notice your breathing. Over 21 thousand times a day you breathe in deeply, and breathe out completely. You are breathing out stress, breathing in peace; breathing out worry, breathing in planning; breathing out anxiety, breathing in harmony, joy. Each breath takes you deeper now, each word takes you deeper.*

*And you might notice your strong, gentle heartbeat, so much slower and deeper than it was just moments ago when we began. Over 86 thousand times a day your heart beats rhythmically, naturally, normally, circulating clean oxygen and nutrients and powerful new ideas from the tips of your fingers to the very soles of your feet. So feel the relaxation flowing from the shoulders to the elbows, from the elbows to the wrists, from the wrists to the tips of the fingers, where you might feel a lightness or a heaviness or even that gentle pulse of relaxation. You are finding ways to appreciate 'old' things in 'new' ways.*

*I wonder what it would be like if the muscles of the neck and shoulders were like heavy ropes coming untied, and just flopping on the floor. The muscles of the neck and shoulders like heavy ropes coming untwined, releasing, letting go, heavy unwound, relaxed. Feeling that wonderful relaxation moving up the neck now, allowing the muscles of the neck to relax, the muscles of the jaw to let go, perhaps allowing the lips to part slightly, as you breathe in deeply and breathe out completely. You are literally becoming a new person as the days go by. You can release, set free, let go of situations, people, events and thoughts.*

*So feel the tiny tendons, the muscles of the cheeks relax; the tiny tendons, the muscles of the forehead relax. Feeling the forehead at peace. They eyelids becoming so heavy, so very heavy it is as though they are locked shut. In fact, you can try to open your eyes and find you cannot, and you go deeper now; try and you cannot and you go deeper now. So easy to relax completely, now. Eyes comfortably closed.*

*You know, some people actually hold stress, strain, even confusion in the tiny muscles of the eyes and forehead. Imagine the possibility of breathing that out.*

*Imagine the possibility of letting that go. Imagine the possibility of the hands and feet actually opening up and all stress, all strain, all confusion, all negative emotion such as anger, shame, guilt, resentment, regret, flowing out of your body. These emotions no longer serve you and you will no longer serve them. They will be removed from your mind, dissolved from your thoughts, eliminated even eradicated from your body's awareness, so free and flexible you simply let them go. You are forgiving, forgetting, and moving on. Forgiving, forgetting, and moving on. So feel the deep relaxation. Everything is not under your control, and that's a very good thing. You are learning to flow with the current and absorb its positive energy throughout your body.*

*So feel the muscles, the tiny tendons of the scalp melt away, the muscles, the tiny tendons of the scalp letting go. So relaxed, so comfortable. Completely at peace. You open yourself up to see the world for what it truly is; you see with clarity and you do not judge what you clearly see, you accept. So feel the body at peace, the mind at peace, the mind and the body at rest. Within you is your healing power; it is safe to be you—you can safely and calmly step into your future.*

*And as you are so very relaxed right now I wonder how relaxed you possibly can be. I wonder if that powerful other-than-conscious of yours is powerful enough to imagine how it would feel if you were as relaxed as you possibly could be as you double your relaxation now.*

*And of course each night as you go to bed it will be so easy to relax completely, so easy to sleep deeply, now.*

*Now, of course you have created your bedroom as a comfortable, serene safe space. Everything comfortably in order—it is so much easier to relax now in a space that is uncluttered and peaceful—just like your powerful mind, serene and peaceful. Naturally 10 or 15 minutes, or even half an hour—after all, you are worth it —20 minutes or so before it is time to drift into peaceful sleep, or more if you like, after all, you are worth it— you can head to your bedroom. As you approach your bedroom you realize this is your time, a time for you to rejuvenate. You are worth it. This is your time to leave behind all the cares, the* concerns, even the devices of the day. You know your bedroom is only for a couple of things, which are deeply fulfilling, and neither of those things involves devices or television or cares, so you have moved all those distractions out of your space, even turning the clock face away from the bed, this is your timeless chamber.

As you approach your bedroom door you know deep inside that this is your time, a time for you to rejuvenate. You are worth it. This is your time to leave behind all the cares, the concerns, even the devices of the day.

It's interesting to know that people forget when they walk through a doorway. We've all walked into another room and wondered exactly why we came in there. In the same way you would walk through a doorway, knowing what was behind you, but simply forgetting about it, just toss it away, throw it away, let it go. Let go of all the cares, the concerns, the devices of the day. Take in a deep breath, all the way down to your diaphragm, feel your shoulders roll back, your chin roll upward, your confidence soar. And step through the door.

This is your time, your space, your place for you. And you are worth it. Absolutely worth it. Worth the time, worth the self-care. As you prepare for bed, brushing your teeth, cleaning, changing, this is your time to change away from the day, your time of renewal and change.

When it is time, when it is absolutely time for you to sleep deeply now, to rest comfortably, you slip comfortably into bed, noticing the way the mattress supports you, beneath your head, beneath your shoulders, beneath your body, just as your powerful other-than-conscious supports the deep rhythm of your breathing over 21 thousand times a day.

As your head touches the pillow and you pull the sheets or blankets over you, you know you will sleep deeply, soundly through the night. Already your thoughts begin to drift, already your dreams begin to flow, already your conscious mind is skipping away to play in the garden of your subconscious thoughts.

And each night, as you go to sleep, you'll sleep so deeply. Even though some days will have problems and things we don't like, each day will be an adventure, and each night is your time to recharge and rejuvenate.

Your brain is an electric device, cycling faster when you are awake—20 cycles a second, and much much slower as you sleep, four cycles, three, even less. And how long does it take to dim a dimmer switch really? To go from a bright hundred watt glow to a lovely beige 15-watt nightlight glow? Tenths of a second, the twinkling of an eye. So easy to cycle down completely, cycling and spiraling, the cycle of your breathing, slower and deeper, spiraling into deep, restful sleep. You will sleep so well.

And as your head touches the pillow and you pull the sheets or blankets over you, you will sleep so soundly. After all your powerful other-than-conscious is always there, always taking care of you. Your ears continue to work of course as you sleep, your other-than-conscious just sorting and filtering anything, so you will hear anything that you need to hear during the night to keep yourself or those with you safe, and the rest your subconscious will simply dismiss. You are listening with your subconscious mind, while your conscious mind is far away and not listening. Your conscious mind is far away and not listening. And you will not mind when your conscious mind skips away to play and dream, because your subconscious mind is always minding things, taking care of you and those with you.

So you can sleep, perchance to dream. And as you lay you down to sleep, you can dream the dreams of your bright, vibrant future, filled with opportunities for health and harmony, joy and happiness. As you dream the dreams, sometimes cycling deeper now, and sometimes sleeping more lightly—

It is natural after all to sleep more lightly and more deeply, to cycle and spiral and flow through the night, and sometime even to be roused. Knowing that if you are roused, you can simply roll over and as your head touches the pillow and you pull the sheets or blankets over you, already your mind and your thoughts begin to flow, deeper now, and you know you simply return to sleep, even deeper now. Even if you are roused to go to the bathroom, you'll find as you quickly return to bed, that as your head touches the pillow and you pull the sheets or blankets over you, already your mind begins to flow now, and you will find that you simply won't recall ever being roused. Simply remembering to forget being roused by forgetting to remember, this will be the one thing you cannot remember. The more you try the more difficult it will be to remember. You will simply awaken feeling you have slept deeply, comfortably through the night.

Perhaps to dream as you cycle through the night. The deep rhythm of your breathing. This is your time to create. This is the time when your creative other-than-conscious— the part of you that is always there and always taking care of you, causing your heart to beat so deeply, slowly now. This is the time when the creative emotional side, the part of you that sees connections you didn't see consciously, that sees possibilities and solutions; this is the time when that creative part of you comes to the fore.

After all you've always known that creativity is not a conscious rational process. Creativity happens when that unconscious part of you sees, feels things you didn't see consciously, and you have those ah-ha! experiences. Those flashes of insight.

Even now as you sleep! your powerful creative unconscious is focused on the things that are truly important in your life, not merely the things that seem to be urgent. This may be the most valuable time of your day so you can allow yourself to sleep. This is the timeless time when your other-than-conscious emotional side, without you even knowing it, is focused on your priorities, the goals to reach your priorities, the action steps to reach your goals, so that you will awaken in the morning at just the right time for you, filled with purpose. Awakening just a minute or two ahead of your alarm, if there is an alarm, awakening in your own time, feeling refreshed.

As you take a deep, dreamy breath, cycling down now, going even deeper. Deeper now. You can sleep because this is some of the most valuable time in your day. This is the time when your body heals, 50 million cells a second, changing and rearranging in the right sequence and order for you. This is the time when your emotions are reset, when mentally you are refreshed. This is your valuable time, your dream time. It is a gift. Your time to rejuvenate and heal.

Perchance to dream. Beautiful dreams. There is simply no time no place no space for the nightmares or night terrors of the past. They simply ride away, flow away. Remembering to forget by forgetting to remember. This is your time to dream beautiful dreams. Your bright future. Perhaps to dream specific steps you are taking, specific changes you are making as you dream your life. Beautiful.

Beautiful dreams, perhaps drifting deeper now, perhaps lighter to discover wonderful lucid dreams— dreams where you somehow know you are dreaming, and as you dream those dreams you can begin to dream the dreams you want, lucid dreams, turning them in the direction you want, creating your own story, your own life. Dreaming your own video game or novel or movie in your mind. Lucid dreams knowing the more you dream the dreams you desire the easier it is to dream the dreams you want to dream. Daydreams at night. Calm relaxed, at peace.

As your head touches the pillow and you pull the sheets or blankets over you, you will sleep so well, so deeply, knowing that in the morning you will awaken feeling refreshed.

And when you awaken in the morning at just the right time for you, you will feel refreshed, full of joy, so eager to get out of bed and greet the morning and get going! You will feel so awake, relaxed, energized; an inner feeling of joy and well being, a feeling of the joy of living. As you greet the day you feel a sense of purpose. Ready to live and create your life. To make powerful specific changes. To live your life to the fullest, making the most of your day, full of energy, vitality.

If this is a time for you to be awake and conscious, then you can return back into the room, feeling perhaps as if you have just had a deep night's sleep. When you are ready to feel particularly good for no particular reason at all, when you are ready to seize the day and make the most of it, when you are ready to feel a sense of joy, then your eyes will open!

*Of course if this is a time for you to sleep! You can let yourself sleep! Deeply now. Taking a deep breath and letting it go. As your head touches the pillow and you pull the sheets or blankets over you, already your mind begins to drift, already your thoughts begin to flow. Already you are beginning to dream beautiful dreams of your bright vibrant future, filled with opportunities for health and harmony, joy and happiness, and knowing that every day, in every way, your life is getting better, your world is getting better, and this is so.*

# 5 THE SURFER
*a metaphor for self-efficacy and control*

"Are you a *Star Trek* fan?" I ask, seemingly àpropos of nothing she's said.

My client paused just a beat, thrown off just a bit by the pattern interrupt. "Not really..."

"Okay then, do you know Chinese finger puzzles?" I offered.

Her brow furrowed.

"Those little woven tubes that you can stick a finger in from each hand, and when you try to pull your fingers apart, the woven tube tightens and binds your fingers so you can't?" I pointed my index fingers at each other, pantomiming the finger trap.

"I see what you're saying," she said. "I've been stuck. Just trying to find one way out."

"Perhaps. Probably," I replied. "But that's not the main problem."

She looked quizzical.

"You've been trying to power out of this mess," I continued. "You've felt you have to have control. The more you try to force the trap, the more stuck you become. It is time for a different solution, a different realization."

She nodded, thinking.

"I remember that quote from *Jurassic Park*, after the dinosaurs are running amok. Ellie Sattler says to John Hammond, the guy who built the park, 'You never had control, that's the illusion!'"

She nodded, her brow creased, her expression is intense. "What were you going to tell me about *Star Trek*?"

"There's a *Next Generation* episode where Captain Picard and the crew find a derelict warship from an ancient battle. It is in the middle of an asteroid field. They go in to take a closer look at the museum piece, and the *Enterprise* gets trapped in the same trap that killed the crew of the ancient starship."

"It turns out," I continued, "That the asteroids held disguised weapons, which drew energy from the ship, and then projected it back as deadly radiation—oh, and also re-directed the ship's power against it, so it couldn't move and escape."

"I'm fueling my own problem," she said. "I keep kicking at this and working at it and it just gets worse and worse."

"It's time for a new approach?" I offered.

"In *Star Trek*, how did they get loose?"

I smiled. "Are you sure you're okay with a spoiler?"

She smiled. "Sure."

I could feel a bit of an emotional difference with her already.

"First they tried force. The *Enterprise* is pretty powerful, of course. But that just made things much worse, since it fueled the weapons and used their own power against them. Then they considered turning the ship over to the computer, on the theory that it could power them out of the trap by making decisions—course adjustments and acceleration—much more quickly than a human could. In the computer simulations the *Enterprise* got out of the asteroid field trap, sometimes."

"But Picard wasn't willing to trust the lives of his crew and his ship to the cold logic of the computer," I continued. "So Picard looks at it another way, tries another approach. Instead of forcing the issue with powerful engines or weapons, he shuts everything off, lets the ship go still and drift. Of course this puts them in danger of the radiation, but that will take a little while to kill them."

She nods.

"Picard himself takes the helm, and orders just one small thrust from a docking jet, just enough to create the tiniest movement forward. The *Enterprise* drifts, accelerating in the gravitation pull of a large asteroid ahead. Picard uses the gravity of the asteroid to slingshot the ship around to a new direction, and guides the ship out of the asteroids and out of danger. Picard compares it to a single pilot flying an old propeller biplane, like in World War I, no instrumentation, just trusting your instincts."

Her gaze at me is intense. "I need to handle this very differently," she says.

## Self-efficacy and learned helplessness

There are a lot of ways to describe mental health, and since it is a good idea to focus on what you want, not on what you don't want, describing health is a very good idea.

One of my favorite descriptions of mental health is self-efficacy. You know that there are things that are outside your control, and you know there are things that you can control. Self-efficacy is the belief that the things in your control tend to determine the nature and quality of your life. You can take meaningful action that will affect what life will be like.

The contrast to self-efficacy is learned helplessness. Learned helplessness is the belief that things outside your control are more important than the things in your control.

The classic (and, in today's context, hugely unethical) behaviorist experiment in learned helplessness was Seligman and Maier's 1960 experiments on dogs. This involved a dog in a large kennel or Skinner box, in which half the floor was wired to provide an electric shock. Naturally, when shocked, the dog would leap to the other side. However, if the dog was tied down and unable to move while shocks were administered, the dog learned helplessness to the point that even if it was untied, it no longer would jump to the shock-free section of the floor.

Any number of Internet memes embody this concept. I've seen photos of a large mule, a thousand-pound animal, tied to a plastic lawn chair weighing no more than a couple of pounds. The idea is that the mule could, of course, drag the chair anywhere, but he doesn't know it. The mule is stuck, because he believes he cannot move. Likewise, there is the meme of the adult elephant held by a rope on the ankle. The five-ton animal could easily break the rope or yank the keeper off his feet, but since the elephant has been raised with the rope from infancy, he believes he cannot get away.

A related narrative involves monkeys in a cage with a ladder and bananas at the top. Whenever a monkey tried to climb the ladder, he was shocked, as were the other monkeys on the floor of the cage. Eventually the monkeys stopped going for the bananas. When new monkeys were introduced to the cage, they were prevented from going after the bananas by the original monkeys. After a time, when all the original monkeys were replaced, the monkeys still prevented each other from climbing up after the bananas. In truth, this experiment was never performed, although the story continues to make the rounds as a science urban legend. True horrors like Seligman and Maier's learned helplessness experiments on dogs and Harlow's truly horrific pit of despair experiments in 1965 on monkeys give sad credence to this sort of tale.

The story rings true not just because of the brutal nature of animal and even human experimentation in the past; the idea that such helplessness and despair can be learned resonates deeply. This is the essence of victimization; it is the goal of the abuser to create the belief in the victim that she or he can do nothing, and can take no action that will help.

This can be the essence of a world view as well. In classical antiquity, people struggled with the concepts of fate and fortune. Fortune meant that things happened to you randomly, by just dumb luck. Fate was no better; certain things were destined to happen, no matter what. In Sophocles' classical play *Oedipus Rex*, Oedipus was doomed to kill his father and marry his mother, no matter what action he took.

The concept of helplessness can run deep in our psyche, both in our culture tales and in our individual stories.

On a day-to-day basis it is not healthy to live as if we are driven by forces outside our control. The belief that you can take meaningful action that will largely determine what your life will be like is the essence of psychological health.

Surfers occurred to me one day as I sought a metaphor to embody this concept. Professional surfers ride monster waves that may even exceed five stories— fifty feet—in height. These monster waves can kill you. They definitely are outside your control. But the surfer does not need to control the wave. He or she only needs to control the board. The metaphor of balancing the board, and the joy and exhilaration of it, strikes me as a wonderful metaphor for self-efficacy. I do not have to control the wave, only balance my life, and ride for the joy of it. Incidentally, I almost titled this metaphor "the wave," but it's not about the wave. It's about the surfer.

I've written this metaphor with a female surfer. I like the idea of a strong woman who is not contented to watch from the beach. If you have a male client, you may want to switch the gender to male, for greater identification and more effective modeling with the surfer.

ജ്ഞയ്ക്കൃ

## The Surfer hypnosis process

*With your eyes comfortably closed, I'd like to invite you to just take a nice, deep breath and slowly let it go. Now I know sometimes it's difficult to relax or to learn how to relax more than you have before.*

*So as you sit there with your eyes closed, comfortable, and begin to become aware of your own sensations I begin to wonder when you've enjoyed the pleasure of sitting on the shore of the ocean. There's something very comforting about just sitting there, listening to the peaceful sound of the waves as they move in and out in a continuous flow that just seems to go on and on. Relaxing in the sun,* feeling the soothing warmth and just letting the mind drift effortlessly with that quiet, almost silent sound in the background of awareness.

Sea foam chasing up onto the shore. I'm not even sure you've done that before, let go and flow, listening to the peaceful quietness of water lapping the shore, daydreaming of a place that is so comfortable and safe that it is easy to allow the mind to relax, the body to relax.

I don't know but I do know that everyone has a place they can go, a relaxing space deep inside where they can really let go of all their cares and concerns and feel the gentle flow of those waves of relaxation, the smooth heaviness of arms and legs as the relaxation continues.

As you continue to breathe deeply and relax, the sand stretches out across a beautiful beach. Down to a cascading, flowing, roaring, surf that is breaking and crashing against the shore. You can see the power of the waves, monstrous, huge, as they flow. Giant waves, feeling the thick sands of Waimea Bay, Hawaii in November, giant waves flowing, cycling, crashing. White, white sea foam spilling up onto the sand. And behind the sea foam the giant rise of the waves blue, huge, beautiful, dangerous, curling.

And you can see the surfer. The surfer out on the board riding far out from shore where the ocean is deep. There is power in the water and you can see the surfer there. She is exciting, challenged, at peace. She takes the tow line from the jet ski that pulls her up onto the mounting wave as it continues to rise high above the level of the sea. And at the right moment, when she's absolutely ready, she simply lets go of the line.

And you can see her there, balanced on the board, gliding across the face of the wave. The power, the flow. That's in the water. And you can see the look on her face, the determination, the fear, the exhilaration, the joy. It's all there. And you realize, this is the challenging moment, the apex experience, for her.

There is no way to control the power of the wave, the flow of the water. It cascades and rushes towards the shore. It will break in foaming sea foam white, splashing, cascading, beating onto the thick sand of the beach.

*But at this moment, at this moment, you can see it there on her face. Alone on the board she's balancing everything. And there's a realization, a moment. The surfer doesn't have to control the power of the wave. The surfer only has to maintain the balance of the board. She shifts her weight with the full use of all her skill, her experience, her training. Her courage. You can tell that she has a sense of excitement, of joy, gliding across the surface of the wave as it begins to curl.*

*And even if you want to see her ride it on in all the way to the conclusion, riding it in on her own terms, safely arriving to the shore like a sea-borne goddess on the cascade of gorgeous foam, you notice as you watch that sometimes —sometimes surfers wipe out.*

*And you can see the surfer there, at that moment, beginning to lose balance. Things happening so quickly, the flash of concern on her face. But as you watch you realize certain things. That for her, it's all been worth it. The exhilaration, the experience, the joy of the ride. Feeling the power of the wave. Every bit of it's worth it. And even though wiping out is potentially very dangerous, you can see this is someone who has wiped out before. She's practiced on smaller waves, probably beginning with 6 or 8 foot waves. She's had that experience of balancing the board. It's taken years of training, dedication, commitment, experience, to develop this level of expertise.*

*She also knows how to fall. To be tumbling in the cascade in the power of the water, and to be all right. And even though it's dangerous and can go really wrong, and even though it's the sort of thing that beats you up a bit, it's still worth it for the exhilaration of the ride. Her safety comes from her own intelligence, experience, strength, balance.*

*And even when she wipes out, there's a gracefulness to it. You can see that this is someone who knows how to handle adversity, who does it very very well. Flowing into the power of the wave. And as the wave washes through and over and you can almost feel your breath caught in your chest, you see her there, emerging, rising over the billowing surface. And you realize, you realize through it, that she's okay. The jet ski comes in the waves, gives her a tow back out to a safer place, calmer waters, beyond the swell of the breakers.*

*But the place of safety is about sitting and watching and waiting for the waves as they arise. Because she's not interested in calling it a day and coming back to the shore. She's there for the joy of living, for the thrill of the experience, for the power of the ride. And soon, you can see her there, taking the tow line from the jet ski, heading up onto another wave of her choosing, ready to feel its power, its beauty, its majesty. The flow and the cascade of the wave. And she doesn't have to control it. She controls the balance on the board. And the balance on the board flows from her inner energy, her inner feeling, the lightness that she has there. There's a contentedness, a sense of peace, in the midst of the curl of the wave, able to enjoy the sense of adventure and to live her life.*

*And you realize as you watch her riding across the face of the wave, her feet balancing the board, her fingers playing in the wall of water that is curling next to her head, that she could just be a girl on the beach, cute in her bathing suit, watching life go by. But that's not who she is. She prefers to live there on the face of the wave. She has a greater feeling of personal well-being, a greater feeling of personal safety and security.*

*She's able to move forward, rapidly, powerfully, finding herself to be so much more happy. You can see it on her face. So much more optimistic. More able to rely upon and depend upon herself, her own efforts, her own judgments, her own opinions. Feeling much less need to have to rely upon, or depend upon, other people.*

*And you realize that she has a sense of emotional calm. Even gliding across the surface of the wave. She has a true perspective where she sees the wave as it is without magnifying or making it bigger in her own mind. You can tell that she has confidence in herself, in her ability to do, not only what she has to do each day, or what she ought to do each day; what she wants to do each day. Without the fear of failure, without the fear of consequences, without unnecessary anxiety. Fear and anxiety are two sides of the same coin. And you can tell that this is* someone who lives to ride. Someone like you, who lives to ride the wave.

Because you could sit on the beach. And you could just watch life just passing by and going by. Or you could allow yourself to paddle out with the board, to feel the power of the wave, to feel the power of life moving around you. There's a deep sense of stability in the core of your being. And even though you have a sense of feeling light inside, buoyant, even contented, there is the part of you that absolutely craves that adventure.

You're not content to watch life go by. No. This is your wave, and this is your moment. You will make your fate, master your destiny. When the time is right, when it is absolutely right for you, you know that you will grab the tow line for the jet ski and ride up onto the face of the wave. And you realize you don't have to control everything that happens around you. You don't have to control all that happens in your life. There are plenty of things that are outside of your control, and no one owes you anything.

But the things that you do control. And the things you control are much more meaningful for your life than are things that are outside of your control. You don't have to control the power of life, the power of the wave; you only have to balance the board and glide and trace your fingers in the water and enjoy. It is who you are. It is simply what you do.

As you're listening to my voice, if this is a time, a place, a space, where you need to be, sleeping deeply, resting comfortably, then you can dream the dreams of life and the power of waves flowing; the sense of adventure of getting out there and getting in it, the cascade and everything playing around you. And in the middle of it all, in the middle of the curl, the sense of well-being, of balance. This is your ride, this is your life, and you're absolutely making the most of it.

Of course, if this is a time when you need to be stepping out into the adventure, grabbing hold of the tow line to ride up onto the wave, making absolutely the most of your day, and living your life with the sense of joy, excitement, adventure—living with only the security that comes from your own being and experience—when you're *ready to live, then at that moment your eyes will open. When your eyes open you will be wide awake, wide awake, feeling wonderful, light, in perfect health, ready for the adventure, realizing of course that every day, in every way, your life is getting better, your world is getting better, and this is so.*

# 6 THE MUSE

*a metaphor for decision making*

It is the solemn ceremony of handshakes.

The pastor stands at the door of the sanctuary at the end of the morning worship service, churchgoers file out, shaking his hand; smiles, friendly greetings ensue.

One man steps up, his face serious, determined. He looks into the pastor's eyes. "That's the best sermon you've ever preached," he says.

The old preacher is taken aback for a moment; that's a big compliment, and it feels intense, completely earnest. "Thank you," he offers. "Please tell me, what touched you so deeply?"

The man's expression is almost far away. "It was where you licked your fingers, turned the page, and said, 'Thus ends part one, it is time to move on to the second part.'" He smiled. "I know what to do now," he says as he walks away, in his own thoughts.

## The emotional unconscious & the rational conscious

The unconscious, which I have come to think of more and more as the emotional side, is a positive force for change, the fountainhead of positive resources and creativity. Unleashed, the emotional side naturally seeks health.

People do not do self-destructive things because they seek self-destructive consequences. Even when something is objectively self-destructive, there is always a private logic that sees the behavior or belief as beneficial. People do not smoke to get cancer or emphysema; they smoke to relieve stress. Likewise, people do not drink excessively because they want to kill someone from behind the wheel, or have extramarital affairs to destroy lives.

To complicate matters even more, an individual may have different, competing emotional reasons battling for control in the unconscious.

The emotional unconscious' impetus to individual actions often don't make sense to the rational conscious of an outsider, or even to the individual in question's sense of cognitive, rational reasoning. But it is critical to understand that the perceived emotional benefits are very real and strongly influence that person's actions.

Of course, the cognitive, rational side of us—the conscious—also has knowledge about what is good for us. Most of us know that it is beneficial to eat appropriate amounts of healthy foods, exercise three times a week, always wear a seat belt in a car, avoid tobacco and change the battery in the smoke detector every six months. Yet millions of people do not take these simple, healthy steps, because knowledge does not have power— it's emotion that runs the show.

People often discuss the need to get the emotional side under conscious control. Although individuals can force themselves to act in ways that are not emotionally comfortable for short periods of time, willpower eventually fails and old habits, driven by powerful unconscious emotions, reassert themselves. It is a mistake to think the cognitive will ever control the emotional, but it is possible to get the two of them on the same course, and to achieve internal harmony. Much of this book is devoted to doing precisely that.

The Muse process is an approach to specifically engage the emotional unconscious as decision maker. Faced with ambivalence or overwhelming choices, often it can be hard to decide what to do, or even whether to do anything at all.

The Muse represents the emotional unconscious, and is a direct invitation to the emotional side to provide a path forward.

The Muse is traditionally a female image, but it doesn't have to be a female figure. You can encourage your client to think in terms of a teacher, coach, mentor or sensei. The Muse represents the emotional, creative self, and can take any form that is comfortable for the client.

"Do you ever listen to the Muse process?" one client asked me.

"Yes, I do," I said.

"What does your Muse look like?" she asked.

"I always get sort of a lovely Grecian goddess type, in a flowing robe," I said.

"That figures," she said. "I get Yoda."

Enjoy the process. I believe it will help you to enable your clients find the creative direction and positive path they need.

ഌ൞ඎ

## The Muse hypnosis process

*As you are relaxing and breathing deeply, eyes closed, and your body is so very comfortable, I'd like to invite you to imagine a beautiful outdoor space. The sort of space where you can step away from everything, peaceful, tranquil, relaxed. You can smell the pleasant fragrance of the forest. Somewhere in the background there is the sound of flowing water, and, perhaps, the faint joyful sound of light laughter, carried on the breeze.*

*As you continue to enjoy this lovely place, you might notice the shushing sound of the breeze in the leaves of the trees, the varying shades of the leaves, and you notice that this place feels very safe and secure. This is in fact your space.*

*As you continue to breathe deeply, allowing your breathing to be full and rhythmic, you find that it is easy to relax completely, to drift down within, and to allow your thoughts to flow, like the sound of the water flowing in the background.*

*You realize this is your space, and you feel a wonderful sense of renewal, a sense or possibility and even purpose here. This is your space, your place, the place where you come to grow, to plan, to move forward.*

*As you begin walking through the woods, noticing perhaps the dappling of the sunlight along the path, and hearing that sound carried through the trees on the breeze, that sound that just might be joyful laughter, you know that ahead there is a place you go for wisdom, for insight; a secret, sacred place deep inside, a beautiful glade beside a deep pool, your own personal sanctuary. And you know that in that space, in your own personal sanctuary, in that beautiful glade by the deep, quiet pool, you will find Wisdom—a coach, a mentor, a wise guide, your very own Muse. You have the sense that you are on a quest, that there are questions, questions that need answers.*

*As you journey through this sylvan wood, feeling absolutely safe and comfortable as this is absolutely your space, noticing, perhaps the variances of color of the leaves, gently moving in the breeze, dappled with enlightening sunlight —you have a sense of expectancy, anticipation.*

*You know that you are coming to a healing, cleansing place. There are so many questions you have, perhaps, and you know you will ask three. You will find the answers you seek. Perhaps you know consciously what you are seeking, or perhaps there is an unconscious part of you seeking this wisdom.*

*Now I don't know if you are on this quest through these faerie woods to find release from something in your past, to resolve something, or to gain insight for this moment today; or perhaps you have a sense that there is something you need to embrace or move forward with.*

Perhaps you even have a sense that there are various paths to different futures, and you are looking for the road to travel. Whether to take the road less traveled or more traveled as the paths diverge. In the woods here you know that you will find just what you need. I don't know if your quest is about something very specific, or something life changing—or perhaps it is both. You know you will find what is right for you, or even best for you. And still in the rustling leaves, just below the level of conscious awareness, there is the faint joy of laughter carried on the breeze, giving you a sense of hope and comfort.

As you come to a knoll, the path rising a bit through massive, majestic trees, part of you knows that this is right for you. That the answers you seek are just beyond the rise, that as you crest the knob you will step into the glade, your sanctuary.

As you ascend to the top, a gorgeous beam of sunlight bursts through the canopy, and shines on you, illuminating you from head to toe, filling you with a feeling of warmth, peace. You can see the lovely glade there before you, and the deep placid pool. Step into this space. Breathe it in, feel it. Notice the beauty of it, the fragrance of gorgeous flowers, of the woods. Notice the feeling of serenity, harmony, peace that flows through your body to the very soles of your feet.

By the pool you can see a familiar place—I don't know if this is a mossy or grassy space to recline, or a solid sturdy and cool stone to rest upon, or even warm sand, inviting by the deep, beautiful pool. But there is a part of you, a powerful other-than-conscious part of you that knows exactly what is best for you, what is right for you, so you can just let that happen. Let that happen now.

As you comfortably sit in this space, you notice your body feels at peace. This is a place of deep healing. After all, that's what your body does best, heal itself at the phenomenal rate of 50 million cells a second, changing and transforming. That is what your powerful other-than-conscious does—constantly creating healing, physically and emotionally.

There is a deep, healing timelessness about this space. And as you are so comfortable here, not knowing if a minute has passed or an hour, just letting your focus flow perhaps into the depths of that beautiful pool, you can hear, faintly, just under your consciousness, the sound of joy, perhaps laughter.

From another space you notice someone stepping or floating into your glade, and you recognize this person to be your Muse.

You see grace and strength, and a quiet calm. As you look into the eyes of your Muse you notice the wisdom, the deep ancient wisdom this Muse has. The intuition.

You recognize this Muse knows everything about you— your past, even things that have slipped from your memory, your desires, your goals, your pain, your dreams. As you see the quiet, joyful smile of the Muse, you know you can absolutely trust this Muse, and the guidance the Muse will give you.

The Muse sits beside you, with you. You feel comforted by the presence of the Muse. Not knowing if a minute has passed or an hour, you realize this is your time. Time for the three questions. You will ask the questions in your mind, in the quiet of this beautiful glade, and the Muse will answer. I don't know if there is something you need to resolve or release or forgive, or if there is something you need to embrace or move forward with—but part of you knows. And in the quiet of this beautiful space you will find the answers you seek. You are open and ready.

Ask the question that is most important to you right now, open and ready to hear. And when my voice returns you will only relax even more deeply, now.
[• Pause 10 seconds]

Deeper now, so as the Muse answers, you may need to know more. Ask your second question. And when my voice returns you will only relax even more deeply, now.
[• Pause 10 seconds]

Deeper now, deep like that placid pool. You may need to know the specific steps you can take that will allow you to release the past or move forward with your future. Ask your third question now. And when my voice returns you will only relax even more deeply, now.
[• Pause 10 seconds.]

*Deeper now, drifting, dreaming, floating flowing, calm, relaxed, at peace. Now you can thank the Muse.*
[● Pause 5 seconds.]

*You can feel strength in the expression on the Muse's face. When you are ready, the Muse walks or floats away. As the Muse leaves, you can hear the joyful sound of the Muse's quiet laughter.*

*You feel centered, focused, here beside the quiet pool in your glade, the place deep inside where you go for wisdom, insight.*

*You have a sense of purpose. Although there may be things beyond your control, you have confidence that you will take meaningful action that will determine what your life will be like.*

*Now, I don't know if a minute has passed or an hour, but when it is the right time for you, you simply walk to that knoll. The bright, warm, comfortable beam of the sun shines down all around you, illuminating your body from your head all the way to the soles of your feet. You are filled with purpose, determination; empowered. You look back at the glade, the quiet pool. You know you can return to this place any time, and you will always find what you seek. Turning forward now, you see the path through the wood stretched out before you. You have the sense that some part of the Muse is with you now. Now is the time to step forward.*

*Now I don't know if this is a time for you to sleep, but if this is a time to sleep, you can carry all this with you into your dreams, where that powerful, creative other-than-conscious part of you will continue to guide you forward. You may dream of specific steps you will take upon awakening that will create your bright future.*

*If this is a time to be awake, alert, conscious, to take action and create, then your eyes will open. When your eyes open you will be filled with purpose, wide awake, and knowing absolutely that every day, in every way, your life is getting better, your world is getting better, and this is so.*

## 7 BEAUTIFUL WINTER
*a metaphor for physical pain alleviation*

Somewhere in the professional's guide to how to write your book, there is probably a section on why it is a bad idea to begin a chapter by telling the story of your greatest clinical failure.

This is particularly true when you are writing about the area where you believe that your process is absolutely the most effective. Yet there was that one day when I felt the failure, and cried in my office.

Physical pain alleviation, in my opinion, is the most powerful thing you can do with hypnosis, and the most likely to succeed. It is a lead-pipe cinch.

My mother has a saying to describe a beautiful young woman: "She still has the dew," the dew of the morning, fresh, when the whole day lies ahead as a beautiful possibility.

This girl definitely had the dew as she walked through my door. It was a spring afternoon, and I could see people through the windows, strolling on Park Street.

She was 16, young and beautiful, as she walked in with her family.

But she moved like an 80-year-old woman. Cautious, guarded, each step taken with great care. I could see the lines too early etched into her face. I glanced at the faces of her parents: her mother's face accustomed to worry, her father's face with a look of grim determination and just a hint of desperation. They unfolded the story.

Two years earlier, on a gorgeous summer day at the beach, Catherine (my client) had fallen off a skim board. In case you're not familiar with these, a skim board is a flat, almost fish-shaped board that young guys and girls sling in front of them into mere inches of sea foam when a wave pounds the beach. They run and jump on it, balancing, the momentum carrying them forward, riding a thin layer of water and foam for only seconds at a time.

Except Catherine didn't glide. She hit the board wrong and drove it into the sand, taking a nasty spill.

But what can go wrong on a day at the beach?

Everything. Because a moment can change your life. Catherine fell wrong, and the consequence, up to that point, were two years of chronic, unrelenting pain.

The family had seen many doctors. As Catherine came in, I could tell she was on painkillers. Her mother told me I was her last hope.

I asked Catherine to rate the pain on the SUDs scale – Subjective Units of Discomfort, the Likert scale from one to 10 to subjectively describe level of pain. Ten is supposed to be incomprehensible. Catherine gave herself an eight.

As I write this, I recall the nine months I spent sitting in a chair or lying on a sofa with pain from the herniated disk in my back. I couldn't stand to be on my feet long enough to walk into a store. I would never say I knew how Catherine felt, but I was familiar with the neighborhood.

We began. Usually clients feel relief from pain after a single session; if the pain has persisted for a while, it may take a few sessions. Sometimes the pain comes back after a few days, so the effect has to be reinforced to make it permanent.

Nine weeks later I had exhausted my knowledge. I never wanted more to be successful with a client. Never. We could knock the pain out, and Catherine moved like the person she truly was, vivacious, 16. But the effect never lasted more than an hour or so following a session. At first this was encouraging, even though it was unusual. If we could get the effect temporarily, surely we could make it more permanent. That is how pain alleviation always works. But not this time. As the weeks went on and we made no more progress, I could feel a growing sense of desperation. I wanted this to work completely.

We completed the therapy; the whole family was again in my office. They were happy. Catherine said that her living level of pain was a three on the SUDs scale.

They left. I began to cry.

Two years later I encountered this family again. Catherine has continued to improve, the acute pain diminishing over time.

## The perception of pain

Since 1995, the US National Institutes of Health (NIH) have strongly recommended hypnosis to treat chronic physical pain. We have known about this effect for a long time. Dr. James Esdale, a Scottish physician in India in the mid-19th century, performed hundreds of surgeries using relaxation as the only anesthetic. This was fortunate for his patients, since the alternatives at the time were basically biting on a piece of leather or the use of beverage alcohol. Although chemical anesthetics (discovered during Esdale's lifetime by another Scottish physician, James Young Simpson) became the medical standard of care, in the early 1990s the NIH was seeking non-medical anesthetic alternatives for cancer patients because of contraindications with chemotherapy drugs.

At the 1990s and previously, we were not sure how processes of hypnosis, functional relaxation, or guided imagery worked to alleviate pain, only that they were very effective. Advances in neuroscience and neuroimaging (brain scans) have allowed us to understand exactly how these processes function.

Hypnotic pain alleviation creates a brain state similar to the one provided by chemical anesthetics, without side effects. Pain is a frontal lobe phenomenon, and hypnotic anesthesia prevents the frontal lobe from processing signals from the body that are perceived as pain. We have already considered how the amygdala processes sensory information and does not alert the cerebral cortex unless there is a need to do so. The same effect is active in hypnotic pain alleviation.

We often think of pain signals from the body as traveling along our nerves in a manner similar to an electrical impulse traveling along a wire, but this metaphor is too simple. It's not as if there is only one wire running from a part of your body to your brain. Neurological signals are sent across the intercellular space (between cells) by neurotransmitters, natural chemicals released by the body. The neurotransmitters do not exclusively affect just the next cell in a line; they spread and can affect many cells, so that the body has a redundant way to send neurological signals, like a branching pathway. These signals move along a complex neural net, and the signals may begin to circle back as neurons reuptake neurotransmitters. When that occurs, it essentially creates a feedback loop in the system, a cycle of pain that may keep cycling and hurting even after an initial injury to the body has healed. Hypnosis is an effective way to interrupt or quiet this looping process.

**Changes in physical experience**

There are many ways to gauge hypnotic depth or suggestibility. The deepest level of hypnosis involves negative hallucination, where the person does not perceive something that is physically present. For example, a person may be hypnotized to believe he is barefoot, and may run around looking for his shoes— even when they are on his feet.

The unconscious continues to be aware of the stimuli, though. If you hypnotize someone and vanish a chair from her perception, she may be confused about how she is sitting on air. But if you ask her to walk across a room when the vanished chair is in her path, she will walk around it. She sees the chair before she does not see it; her unconscious is keeping her safe, while her conscious remains unaware of the obstruction. If you ask her why she walked around the area where the chair is, she will create a rationalization to explain, something like, "I just wanted to look at the painting on the wall instead of walking across the middle of the room."

This illustrates an important point as to why *why* questions are not a good idea in therapy. They pull people away from core emotional realities, and invite cognitive rationalization (which can create further problems such as the creation of retroactive causes, which we discussed in Chapter 1).

Pain is just one of many physical perceptions, though. Any imaginable physical sensation can be created using hypnosis. Hypnosis can be used to cool hot flashes following menopause. The use of sexual imagery to create arousal and orgasm can be helpful for people who experience different types of sexual dysfunction, including non-physical erectile dysfunction, premature ejaculation, lack of libido, and difficulties engaging in healthy sexual relations following sexual trauma. The perceived ear ringing of tinnitus can be reduced with hypnotic processes.

**Medical Diagnosis**

Proper medical diagnosis and treatment by a physician must be obtained, and the anesthetic, not healing, nature of pain alleviation must be understood by the client.

There are many different ways to create physical pain relief, and I provided a different approach in the book *Emotion the Power of Change*. Whatever approach is used, however, it is critical that the pain first be diagnosed by a qualified physician. As stated earlier, pain is a warning system, an alarm that something is wrong and needs attention. The problem needs to be clearly understood so that it can be properly addressed and medically treated.

Whether healing has occurred or not. chronic or debilitating pain needs to be addressed and relieved. It is important for the client to understand that hypnotic pain alleviation does not heal the body; the process is an anesthetic. It is critical that the client clearly understand that activities that may cause further injury *still* may cause further injury, even though the pain has been relieved.

ഇ൴ഁഃ

## The Beautiful Winter hypnosis process

As you are just relaxing, breathing deeply, noticing the gentle sensations of relaxation, soothing, peaceful, I'd like to invite you to take a nice full, comfortable breath, and slowly let it go.

And another nice, full soothing breath, and slowly let it go, feeing a sense of relief, feeling the mind at rest, the body at rest, the mind and the body at peace.

And as you relax deeply today, this is a time to feel relief, to let go, and flow. Now the reality is that pain, discomfort, is not bad or wrong, it is your body's way of letting you know that something needs attention, help. So I would like you to be 100 percent sure that you and your physician understand the discomfort we are about to relieve, and you can feel very comfortable now letting go of it now, because you know are not interfering with any messages your body needs to send you and it feels fine to just let this go now.

So as you allow your breathing to be so smooth and fine, noticing the gentle, comfortable sensations of relaxation flowing through your body, soothing, you know you can relax even more deeply now if you think of a beautiful place. If you let yourself experience a beautiful, comforting place; if you step into it and breathe it in, allowing yourself to be in that relaxing, beautiful place.

So I would like to invite you to think of a beautiful winter place, like the mountains in winter, or perhaps a ski resort. Breathe it in, feel it, be there—the white white snow flowing over the ground, covering the branches of the trees, deep and crisp and even. All is calm, all is bright and beautiful. You can see your breath, and the beautiful winterscape before you is almost magical.

Now, as you can see your breath, so numbing cold and crisp, I don't know if the sky is that beautiful deep winter blue, which is so vivid, with a white white low winter sun. Or if it is the deep gray of beautiful low overcast clouds, portending more snow, leaving the light muted and gossamer, and perhaps misty gray and peaceful. But there is a part of you, a powerful, other-than-conscious part of *you that knows exactly what's best for you, exactly what's right for you, exactly what's most comforting for you, so you can just let that happen. Let that happen now.*

*Everything is magical and peaceful, and preternaturally quiet, at peace.*

*And as you can see the cold white white winter snow, deep and crisp and even, you can feel the breeze, a cold winter wind, blowing against your forehead, making your temples colder and colder and colder and colder and more numb. Imagine or experience—see!—the blood vessels of the head being cooled and soothed by the lovely cold, returning to their natural, normal color. Feel the soothing cold blowing through your body wherever you need it, extinguishing any inflammation, soothing, cooling, healing, comforting your body.*

*Feel the deep sense of relief as you know your body is constantly healing itself. After all, that's what your body does best, heal itself at the phenomenal rate of 50 million cells a second, changing and rearranging in the right sequence and the right order for you. And right now your body's healing energies are focusing wherever you need that deep healing, as that cold winter wind flows through you, creating deep relief, numbness.*

*Of course the white white blood cells are there to protect and heal the body, to fight off foreign invaders and mutant cells, so you can feel the white white blood cells now, leaving any tissues of the body in peace. The body itself soothing and smoothing and healing and comforting, extinguishing any inflammation, allowing the tissues of the body to return to their natural, normal, healthy color and texture.*

*As you look out across the white white snow, deep and crisp and even, flowing over the landscape, covering the boughs of the trees, feeling that cold cold winter's breeze, you can create that numb comfortable sensation anywhere you need it.*

*As you begin to walk through the snow, deep and crisp and even, you notice that your body moves, easily, fluidly, effortlessly, comfortably. Feel the comfort as your body moves. There is an almost heavenly peace, and you can hear the gentle tink of white white snowflakes, against your coat, falling from the sky or perhaps blown by the cold, numbing winter's wind, which almost seems to blow through you.*

*You come to a beautiful mountain stream, and you can see the water flowing crystal cold and beautiful. Icicles cascade from the spray of the water flowing over the rocks, and you can see the ice on the stones at the edge of the stream, like glass, so cold and so beautiful.*

*You reach down and plunge your hand into the cold cold water, as your hand immediately goes comfortably, completely totally numb.*

*It does not matter how you create this numb sensation or how your subconscious does it for you. The only thing that is important now is that you know you can create this numb, comfortable sensation, any time, any place you want to, simply by closing your eyes and breathing deeply, experiencing that white white snow flowing in your mind.*

*As your hand goes comfortably numb, you may notice just how warm and comfortable your feet feel in your boots, or you might notice some other place in your body that feels very comfortable, allowing all your awareness, and the warmth of your blood, to flow there. You are focusing on what you want, not on what you don't want; focusing on what feels good now.*

*After all it is easy to create that numb lack of sensation —your body does it all the time. You are usually not aware of the sensation of the fabric of your shirt, or of your shoes on your feet. So much sensory information comes in all the time that you can't possibly process it all consciously. Your powerful other-than-conscious experiences and sorts all that, and lets you feel only what is important for you, only what is beneficial for you. You are feeling with your subconscious mind, while your conscious mind is far away and doing other things. And, mind you, your subconscious mind is minding everything so that your conscious mind will not mind as your subconscious mind minds things for you and takes care of you, creating that numb sensation any time you need it, anywhere you need it.*

*White white snow, drifting and flowing and blowing. Beautiful. Numbing, anesthetic, comfortable. At peace.*

*As you walk through the beautiful white white snow, noticing how easily, how effortlessly and comfortably your body moves, you come to a beautiful place, which you recognize as your place. It feels comfortable, like home. Now I don't know if this is a rustic mountain cabin, a beautiful ski lodge, or a gorgeous mountain chalet, but your powerful other-than-conscious knows exactly what's best for you, exactly what's right for you, exactly what's most comfortable for you.*

*It's interesting to know that people forget when they walk through a doorway. We've all walked into another room, into another place, and wondered exactly why we came in there. You can walk through a doorway, knowing what was behind you, but simply forgetting about it. As you step up to this door, the door to your space, you can feel how good your body feels. Feel your shoulders roll back, your chin roll upward, your confidence soar. This is the time to leave behind any discomfort of the past as you step through the door now.*

*As you step into this warm, beautiful space, feeling a deep sense of peace and comfort, perhaps enjoying the lovely fragrance of spruce or pine or cedar, you realize that here you feel absolutely safe, totally comfortable, completely at peace. You can see the white white snow beautiful through the windows.*

*As you come into your space, this is the time to just let everything go, and slip into a nice, warm, soothing bath. You can feel the warm water covering your entire body, up to your neck, and you can feel your body, comfortable, floating, weightless in the soothing water.*

*As you turn on the hot water to make the bath hotter and hotter, your temples are becoming colder and colder, and more numb. You know there is deep healing in your body. This is your time to drift and float and flow.*

*When it is perfectly time, you open the drain, allowing any remaining discomfort to flow away, leaving your body soothed and comfortable. Feel the deep relief, the comfortable numbness.*

*As you dry off and slip into something comfortable, you begin to walk through your space, your cabin or lodge or chalet. White white snow is deep and crisp and even and beautiful outside the windows.*

*You come to a door, and as you open it you realize this is the electrical closet, the nerve center of the house. You can see the fuse box, each switch clearly labeled, for each part of the body. One for the right foot, one for the hip, one for the back, one for the left shoulder, one for the right arm, one for the head, and one for every other place on the body. And you can see the wires going to those switches, the nerves that carry sensation all going through those switches. You can reach up and flip those switches to the greatest position of comfort, and then no sensation can get through there, no sensation at all, because you've turned those switches there.*

*As you step into the bedroom, which you recognize as a place you've created for yourself of peace and comfort and healing, you can see the white white snow out the windows, in the waning early evening beautiful winter light. Perhaps a white white moon floats peacefully above snow-capped peaks. You realize that here in these winter mountains that you are on top of the world. You are absolutely on top of the world.*

*As you slip comfortably into bed, as your head touches the pillow and you pull the sheets or blankets up over you, this is your time to sleep, to dream to flow. Beautiful, healing dreams.*

*This is the time when your powerful other-than-conscious allows your body to go comfortably, completely, totally numb, fading away, gone from your mind, gone from your thoughts, gone from your experience. This is the time when your body heals itself, 50 million cells a second, creating deep healing. The mind at rest, the body at rest, the mind and the body at peace. Comfortable.*

*As you are listening to my voice, if this is a time when you need to be awake and conscious, you can begin the process of coming back into the room. When you awaken you know you will feel refreshed and good! As you come back into the room you may not even notice that you keep the lack of sensation of comfortable numbness anywhere you need it. As you come into the room, feeling a healing energy moving through your body that feels so very good, you may notice just how good your hands or feet or some other healthy part of your body feels now. Focusing all your attention on how good that healthy part of your body feels now.*

*When you are ready to feel particularly good for no particular reason at all, then your eyes will open, you will be wide awake, wide awake feeling fine in perfect health, feeling so much better than before.*

*Of course if this is a time for you to sleep! to rest, to heal to dream, you can let that happen now. Just take a comfortable breath, slowly let it go. As your head touches the pillow and you pull the sheets or blankets over you, already your body simply dissolves away, gone from your thoughts, your mind even your awareness. This is your time to sleep, to heal, to fade away comfortable. Sleeping in that bedroom under that beautiful winter moon glistening through the window over white white winter snow, and comfortably knowing that every day, in every way, your life is getting better, your world is getting better, and this is snow.*

# DÉNOUEMENT

Rachel looked at me and smiled, which was an amazing thing. Six weeks earlier we began working to relieve her chronic, debilitating pain that she suffered after an automobile accident six years ago.

In her 30s, she moved cautiously when she first came in. Her face was drawn, and I could see the presence of the painkillers, which were clearly not helping enough.

Now she moved easily, lightly, beautifully. She smiled.

"Maybe you can help me with my bipolar," she said.

"What bipolar?" I asked. That had not emerged yet in our conversations—we had been very focused on relieving the pain—but today she decided to open up a bit more.

"I've been bipolar for six years," she said.

"Bipolar one or bipolar two?" I asked.

"Bipolar two."

I remembered the old mnemonic: Bipolar one has more fun, bipolar two feels more blue. Her issue was on the depression, not the manic, side.

"The upswings—do you do anything that is really over the top, spending lots of money you don't have, being so active it annoys your friends, having random sex you regret later—that sort of thing?" I ask, trying to gauge the presence of manic episodes.

She shakes her head. "No, never anything remotely like that – I was just happy."

"So what you're telling me is that for the last six years you've been mostly depressed, and occasionally you would swing up out of that and just feel happy, but you couldn't maintain it, right?" I offer.

"Yes."

"So what you're telling me is that for the last six years, since the car wreck, you've been mostly depressed while you were in chronic pain. Occasionally you would swing up out of that, because that is not who you are at your core, but you couldn't maintain it because of the pain. Is that about right?"

"I'm not bipolar," she said, realization washing over her face as a different reality dawned.

# BIBLIOGRAPHY

## Why You Should Buy This Book Now

Hoffman, L. (1990). Constructing realities: An art of lenses. *Family Process, 29*(1), 1-12.

Howard, G.S. (1991). Culture tales: A narrative approach to thinking, cross-cultural Psychology, and Psychotherapy. *American Psychologist, 46*(3), 187-197.

Howard, G.S. (1989). *A tale of two stories: Excursions into a narrative approach to psychology.* Notre Dame, IN: Academic.

## Forward

Barry, D. (n.d.) A million words. *The Miami Herald.* Retrieved from http://www.davebarry.com/natterings_files/dave MILLIONWORDS.pdf. Available in Barry, D. (1997). *Greatest Hits.* New York: Ballantine Books.

Barry, D. (1993). *Bad Habits.* New York: Holt Paperbacks.

Jennings, L., & Skovholt, T. M. (1999). The cognitive, emotional, and relational characteristics of master therapists. *Journal of Counseling Psychology, 46*(1), 3-11.

## Front Quotes

Epictetus, first century CE, *The Enchiridion.*

Hampson, J. (2000). If I am [Recorded by Nine Days]. On *The Madding Crowd* [CD]. New York: 550 Music.

Milton, J. (1667/1674). *Paradise Lost*, Book 1.

Nicks, S. (1975). Rhiannon [Recorded by Fleetwood Mac]. On *Fleetwood Mac* [album]. Van Nuys, CA: Reprise Records. (1976).

Rowling, J. K. (2007). *Harry Potter and the deathly hallows.* New York: Scholastic.

Shakespeare, W. (1599/1601). *The Tragedy of Hamlet, Prince of Denmark*, Act II Scene 2.

Svensson, P., & Persson, N. (1995). Lovefool [Recorded by The Cardigans]. On *First Band on the Moon* [album]. Stockholm, Sweden: Stockholm Records. (1996).

## Chapter 1: Solutions & the Source of Change

Belli, R. F., Winkieman, P., Read, J. D., Schwarz, N., & Lynn, S. J. (1998). Recalling more childhood events leads to judgments for poorer memory: Implications for the recovered/false memory debate. *Psychonomic Bulletin & Review, 5*(2), 318-323.

Campbell, R., Martin, C., & Fabos, B. (2010). *Media and culture: An introduction to mass communications.* Boston: Bedford/St. Martin's.

De Shazer, S. (1997). Radical acceptance. *Family Systems and Health, 15*, 375-378.

Erickson, M. H., & Rossi, E. L. (ed). (1980).*The nature of hypnosis and suggestion* (collected papers of Milton H. Erickson, vol. 1). Irvington Publishers. Retrieved from https://www.scribd.com/doc/11320394/Erickson -Collected-Papers-Vol1

Feldman, J. B. (1985). The work of Milton Erickson: A multisystem model of eclectic therapy. *Psychotherapy, 22*, 154-162.

Freud, S. (1933). *New introductory lectures on psychoanalysis.*

Gruzelier, J. H. (2006). Frontal functions, connectivity and neural efficiency underpinning hypnosis and hypnotic susceptibility. *Contemporary Hypnosis, 23*(1), 15-32.

Gruzelier, J., Gray, M. & Horn, P. (2002). The involvement of frontally modulated attention in hypnosis and hypnotic susceptibility: Cortical evoked potential evidence. *Contemporary Hypnosis, 19*(4), 179-189.

Hupbach, A., Hartz, O., Gomez, R., & Nadel, L. (2008). The dynamics of memory: Context-dependent updating. *Learning & Memory, 15*, 574-579.

Hurd, G. A.. (Producer), & Cameron, J. (Director). (1984). *The Terminator* [Motion picture]. USA: Orion Pictures.

James, G. (2014). Use neuroscience to remain calm under pressure. *Inc.* Retrieved from http://www.inc.com/geoffrey-james/use-neuroscience-to-remain-calm-under-pressure.html?RedirectMobile=false

Jamieson, G.A., & Sheehan, P.W. (2004). An empirical test of Woody and Bowers's dissociated control theory of hypnosis. *The International Journal of Clinical and Experimental Hypnosis, 52*(3), 232-249.

Kirsch, I., & Lynn, S. J. (1995). The altered state of hypnosis: Changes in the theoretical landscape. *American Psychologist, 50*(10), 846-858.

Knapton, S. (2014, July 22). Lack of sleep implants 'false' memories in brain. *The Telegraph*. Retrieved from http://www.telegraph.co.uk/science/science-news/10983097/Lack-of-sleep-implants-false-memories-in-brain.html

Ksir, C., Hart, C. L. & Ray, O. (2009). *Drugs, society, and human behavior*. New York: McGraw-Hill.

Laney, C., & Loftus, E. F. (2008). Emotional content of true and false memories. *Memory, 16*(5), 500-516.

Lilenfeld, S. O., & Arkowitz, H. (2009). Is hypnosis a distinct form of consciousness? *Scientific American*. Retrieved from http://www.scientificamerican.com/article.cfm?id=is-hypnosis-a-distinct-form

Lindsay, D. S., Hagen, L., Read, J. d., Wade, K. A., & Garry, M. (2004). True photographs and false memories. *Psychological Science, 15*(3), 149-154.

Maslow, A. (1962). *Toward a psychology of being*.

Matthews, R. (1992). How one in five have given up smoking. *New Scientist, 1845*, 6.

Media Giants. (2001). *Frontline*. Retrieved from http://www.pbs.org/wgbh/pages/frontline/shows/cool/giants/

Miller, W. (1998). Toward a motivational definition and understanding of addiction. MI Nordic. Retrieved from http://www.motiverandesamtal.org/miwiki/Toward%20a%20Motivational%20Definition

Miller, W. R., & Rollnick, S. (2002). *Motivational interviewing: Preparing people for change* (2nd ed.). New York: The Guilford Press.

Nickerson, R. S. (1998). Confirmation bias: A ubiquitous phenomenon in many guises. *Review of General Psychology, 2*(2), 175-220.

Nourkova, V., Bernstein, D. & Loftus, E. (2004). Altering traumatic memory. *Cognition & Emotion, 18*(4), 575-585.

Ortigue, S., Bianchi-Demicheli, F., Patel, N., Frum, C., & Lewis, J. W. (2010). Neuroimaging of love: fMRI meta-analysis evidence toward new perspectives in sexual medicine. *Journal of Sexual Medicine, 7*(11), 3541-3552.

Roven, C., Thomas, E., Franco, L. (Producers), & Nolan, C. (Director). (2005). *Batman Begins* [Motion picture]. USA: Warner Brothers Pictures.

Stocks, J. T. (1998). Recovered memory therapy: A dubious practice technique. *Social Work, 43*(5), 423 - 436.

Schjoedt, U., Stødkilde-Jørgensen, H., Geertz, A.W., Lund, T.E., & Roepstorff, A. (2009). The power of charisma – perceived charisma inhibits the frontal executive network of believers in intercessory prayer. *Social Cognitive and Effective Neuroscience, 4*, 199-207. Retrieved from http://scan.oxfordjournals.org/content/early/201 0/03/12/scan.nsq023.full.pdf+html

Sommer, C. (1992). *Conversational hypnosis: A manual of indirect suggestion.* Downers Grove, IL: Sommer Solutions, Inc.

Syracuse University (2010, October 25). Falling in love only takes about a fifth of a second, research reveals. *ScienceDaily.* Retrieved from http://www.sciencedaily.com- /releases/2010/10/101022184957.htm

Talbot, M. (2001). The lives they lived: 01-07-01: Peggy McMartin Buckey, b. 1926; The devil in the nursery. *The New York Times.* Retrieved from http://www.nytimes.com/2001/01/07/magazine/

lives-they-lived-01-07-01-peggy-mcmartin-buckey-
b-1926-devil-nursery.html

Turner, E. H., Matthews, A. M., Linardatos, E., Tell, R. A.,
& Rosenthal, R. (2008). Selective publication of
antidepressant trials and its influence on apparent
efficacy. *The New England Journal of Medicine,
358*(3), 1533-4406.

Vesely, A. (Director). (n.d.). *Wizard of the Desert* [Motion
picture]. USA: Noetic Films. Available from
http://wizardofthedesertmovie.com

Viswesvaran, C., & Schmidt, F.L. (1992). A meta-analytic
comparison of the effectiveness of smoking
cessation methods. *Journal of Applied Psychology,
77*(4), 554-561.

Wessel, I., & Wright, D. (2004). Emotional memory
failures: On forgetting and reconstructing
emotional experiences. *Cognition & Emotion, 18*(4),
449-455.

Zhu, B., Chen, C., Loftus, E. F., Lin, C., He, Q., Chen, C.,
Xue, G., Lu, Z., & Dong,Q. (2010). Individual
differences in false memory from misinformation:
Cognitive factors. *Memory, 18*(5), 543-555.

Zoellner, L. A., Foa, E. B., Brigidi, B. D., & Przeworski, A.
(2000). Are trauma victims susceptible to "false
memories?" *Journal of Abnormal Psychology,
109*(3), 517-524.

**Chapter 2: The Three Doors**

Andrews, P. W., & Thomson, J. A. (2009). The bright side
of being blue: Depression as an adaptation for
analyzing complex problems. *Psychological Review,
116*(3), 620–654.

Cytowic, R. E. (n.d.). What percentage of your brain do
you use? TED Ed Lessons Worth Sharing.
Retrieved from http://ed.ted.com/lessons/what-
percentage-of-your-brain-do-you-use-richard-e-
cytowic#review

Frankl, V. (1959). *Man's Search for Meaning.*

Lehrer, J. (2010, February 25). Depression's upside. *The
New York Times.* Retrieved from

http://www.nytimes.com/2010/02/28/magazine/
28depression-t.html?pagewanted=1

Radvansky, G., & Copeland, D. E. (2006). Walking through doorways causes forgetting: Situation models and experienced space. *Memory & Cognition, 34*(5), 1150-1156.

Radvansky, G., Krawietz, S. A., & Tamplin, A. K. (2011). Walking through doorways causes forgetting: Further explorations. *The Quarterly Journal of Experimental Psychology, 64*(8), 1632-1645.

**Chapter 3: Fading Photographs**

Baskin, T. W., & Enright, R. D. (2004). Intervention studies on forgiveness: A meta-analysis. *Journal of Counseling & Development, 82*, 79 – 90.

Boyer, M. F. (2001). Matching hypnotic interventions to pathology types: A working model for expressive psychotherapies. *International Journal of Clinical and Experimental Hypnosis, 49*, 352-360.

Corey, G. (2012). *Theory and practice of counseling and psychotherapy*. Belmont, CA: Brooks/Cole Publishing Company.

Farrow, T. F. D., Zheng Y., Wilkinson, I. D., Spence, S. A., Deakin, J. F., Tarrier N., Griffiths, P. D., & Woodruff, P. W. R. (2001) Investigating the functional anatomy of empathy and forgiveness. *NeuroReport, 8*, 2433–2438.

Greenberg, L. J., Warwar, S. H., & Malcolm, W. M. (2008). Differential effects of emotion-focused therapy and psychoeducation in facilitating forgiveness and letting go of emotional injuries. *Journal of Counseling Psychology, 55*, 185-196.

LeRoy, M. (Producer), & Felming, V. (Director). (1939). *The Wizard of Oz* [Motion picture]. USA: Metro-Goldwyn-Mayer.

Reed, H., Burkett, L., & Garzon, F. (2001). Exploring forgiveness as an intervention in psychotherapy. *Journal of Psychotherapy in Independent Practice, 2*(4), 1-16.

Reeve, J. (2009). *Understanding motivation and emotion.* (5th ed.). Hoboken, NJ: Wiley.

Sullivan, M.F., Skovholt, T.M., & Jennings, L. (2005). Master therapist's construction of the therapy relationship. *Journal of Mental Health Counseling, 27*(1), 48-70.

Walton, E. (2005). Therapeutic forgiveness: Developing a model for empowering victims of sexual abuse. *Clinical Social Work Journal, 33,* 193-207.

**Chapter 4: Sleep!**

Cojan, Y., Waber, L., Schwartz, S. Rossier, L., Foster, A., & Vuilleumier, P. (2009). The brain under self-control: Modulation of inhibitory and monitoring cortical networks during hypnotic paralysis. *Neuron, 62,* 862-875.

Cojan, Y., Waber, L., Carruzzo, A., & Vuilleumier, P. (2009). Motor inhibition in hysterical conversion paralysis. *NeuroImage, 47,* 1026–1037.

Duke, A. (2013, June 24) Expert: Michael Jackson went 60 days without real sleep. CNN. Retrieved from http://www.cnn.com/2013/06/21/showbiz/jackson-death-trial

Hegarty, S. (2012, February 22). The myth of the eight-hour sleep. *BBC News Magazine.* Retrieved from http://www.bbc.com/news/magazine-16964783

*Insufficient sleep Is a public health epidemic.* (2013, March 14). Centers for Disease Control and Prevention. Retrieved from: http://www.cdc.gov/features/dssleep/

*Integration of behavioral and relaxation approaches into the treatment of chronic pain and insomnia.* (1995, October 16-18). Technology Assessment Conference Statement (pp. 1-34). National Institutes of Health. Retrieved from: http://consensus.nih.gov/1995/1995BehaviorRelaxPainInsomniata017html.htm

Konnikova, M. (2013, December 10). Snoozers are, in fact, losers. *The New Yorker.* Retrieved from http://www.newyorker.com/tech/elements/snoozers-are-in-fact-

losers?utm_source=tny&utm_campaign=generalsoc
ial&utm_medium=facebook

Murdock, K. K. (2013). Texting while stressed:
Implications for students' burnout, sleep, and well-
being. *Psychology of Popular Media Culture.*

Painter, K. (2014, March 7). Sleeping pill use rises as
risky patterns emerge. *USA Today.* Retrieved from
http://www.usatoday.com/story/news/nation/20
14/03/07/sleeping-pill-risk/6078041/

Philipson, A. (2013, November 13). Computers and
phones in children's bedrooms 'can cause anxiety
and sleep loss.' *The Telegraph.* Retrieved from
http://www.telegraph.co.uk/education/education
news/10448123/Computers-and-phones-in-
childrens-bedrooms-can-cause-anxiety-and-sleep-
loss.html

Reddy, S. (2014, July 21). Why seven hours of sleep
might be better than eight: Sleep experts close in
on the optimal night's sleep. *The Wall Street
Journal.* Retrieved from
http://online.wsj.com/articles/sleep-experts-
close-in-on-the-optimal-nights-sleep-
1405984970?mod=WSJ_hppMIDDLENexttoWhats
NewsSecond

Stockton, C. (2014, January 3). 15 people on their
experience with the 'sleep paralysis demon.'
*Thought Catalog.* Retrieved from
http://thoughtcatalog.com/christine-
stockton/2014/01/15-people-on-their-experience-
with-the-sleep-paralysis-demon/

Thakkar, V. G. (2013, April 27). Diagnosing the wrong
deficit. *The New York Times.* Retrieved from
http://www.nytimes.com/2013/04/28/opinion/s
unday/diagnosing-the-wrong-
deficit.html?pagewanted=all&_r=0

Washington and Lee University. (2013, September 26).
Study links heavy texting, sleep problems in
college freshmen. *ScienceDaily.* Retrieved from
www.sciencedaily.com/releases/2013/09/130926
111901.htm

## Chapter 5: The Surfer

Kennedy, K., Molen, G. R. (Producers), & Spielberg, S. (Director). (1993). *Jurassic Park* [Motion picture]. USA: Universal Pictures.

Maggie (2008, September 7). Top 10 unethical psychological experiments. *Listverse*. Retrieved from http://listverse.com/2008/09/07/top-10-unethical-psychological-experiments/

Maestripieri, D. (2012). What monkeys can teach us about human behavior: From facts to fiction. *Psychology Today*. Retrieved from http://www.psychologytoday.com/blog/games-primates-play/201203/what-monkeys-can-teach-us-about-human-behavior-facts-fiction

Roman, R., Piller, M., Danus, R. Watner, M. I.. (Writers), & Beaumont, G. (Director). (1989). Booby trap [Television series episode]. In G. Roddenberry (Producer), *Star Trek: The Next Generation*. Hollywood, CA: Paramount Domestic Television.

## Chapter 6: The Muse

No references. Just enjoy!

## Chapter 7: Beautiful Winter

Arons, H. (1961). *New master course in hypnotism*. Irvington, NJ: Power Publishers.

Aung, H. H., Dey, L., Rand, V., & Yuan, C. (2004). Alternative therapies for male and female sexual dysfunction. *The American Journal of Chinese Medicine, 32*(2), 161–173.

Baylor University. (2012, October 31). Clinical hypnosis can reduce hot flashes after menopause. *ScienceDaily*. Retrieved from www.sciencedaily.com/releases/2012/10/121024111526.htm

Baylor University. (2014, July 10). Men's hot flashes: Hypnotic relaxation therapy may ease the discomfort that guys don't talk about. *ScienceDaily*. Retrieved from

www.sciencedaily.com/releases/2014/07/140710
081045.htm

Baylor University. (2013, August 15). Sexual health for postmenopausal women improved by hypnotic relaxation therapy. *ScienceDaily.* Retrieved from www.sciencedaily.com/releases/2013/08/130815 172342.htm

Benedetti, F., Mayberg, H. S., Wager, T. D., Stohler, C. S., & Zubieta, J. (2005). Neurobiological mechanisms of the placebo effect. *The Journal of Neuroscience, 25*(45), 10390 –10402.

Berner, M., & Günzler, C. (2012), Efficacy of psychosocial interventions in men and women with sexual dysfunctions — A systematic review of controlled clinical trials. *Journal of Sexual Medicine, 9*(12), 3089–3107.

Crawford, H.J., Gur, R.C., Skolnick, B., Gur, R.E., & Benson, D.M. (1993). Effects of hypnosis on regional cerebral blood flow during ischemic pain with and without suggested hypnotic analgesia. *International Journal of Psychophysiology, 15,* 181-195.

Elkins, G. R., Fisher, W. I. Johnson, A. K., Carpenter, J. S., & Keith, T. Z. (2013). Clinical hypnosis in the treatment of postmenopausal hot flashes : a randomized controlled trial. *Menopause: The Journal of The North American Menopause Society,* 20(3), 291-8.

Elkins, G. R., Kendrick, C., & Koep, L. (2014). Hypnotic relaxation therapy for treatment of hot flashes following prostate cancer surgery: A case study. *International Journal of Clinical and Experimental Hypnosis, 62*(3), 251.

Faymonville, M.E., Laureys, S., Degueldre, C., Fiore, G.D., Luxen, A. Franck, G., Lamy, M., & Maquet, P. (2000). Neural mechanisms of antinociceptive effects of hypnosis. *Anesthesiology, 92,* 1257–1267. Retrieved from http://journals.lww.com/anesthesiology/toc/2000 /05000

Hamill, K. (2011). The orgasm whisperer. *Marie Claire, 18*(1), 67.

*Integration of behavioral and relaxation approaches into the treatment of chronic pain and insomnia.* (1995, October 16-18). Technology Assessment Conference Statement (pp. 1-34). National Institutes of Health. Retrieved from: http://consensus.nih.gov/1995/1995BehaviorRelaxPainInsomniata017html.htm

Krane, E. (2011) The mystery of chronic pain. TED Talk. Retrieved from http://www.ted.com/talks/elliot_krane_the_mystery_of_chronic_pain

Lynn, S. J. (2007). Hypnosis and the treatment of posttraumatic conditions: An evidence-based approach. *International Journal of Clinical and Experimental Hypnosis, 55*(2), 167-188.

Peebles-Kleiger, M. J. (1989). Using countertransference in the hypnosis of trauma victims: A model for turning hazard into healing. *American Journal of Psychotherapy, 43*(4), 518-530.

Ploghaus, A., Tracey, I., Gati, J.S., Clare, S., Menon, R.S., Matthews, P.M. Nicholas, J., & Rawlins, P. (1999). Dissociating pain from its anticipation in the human brain. *Science, 284*, 1979-1981.

Poon, M. W. (2007). The value of using hypnosis in helping an adult survivor of childhood sexual abuse. *Contemporary Hypnosis, 24*(1), 30-37.

Schulz-Stübner, S., Krings, T., Meister, I., Rex, S., Thron, A., & Rossaint, R. (2004). Clinical hypnosis modulates functional magnetic resonance imaging signal intensities and pain perception in a thermal stimulation paradigm. *Regional Anesthesia & Pain Medicine, 29*, 549-556.

Zubieta, J, Smith, Y. R., Bueller, J. A., Xu, Y., Kilbourn, M. R., Jewett, D. M. Meyer, C. R., Koeppe, R. A., & Stohler, C. S. (2001). Regional mu opioid receptor regulation of sensory and affective dimensions of pain. *Science, 293*(5528), 311-315.

**Excerpt from *Emotion: The Power of Change***

Erickson, M.H., & Rossi, E.L. (1975). Varieties of Double Bind. *The American Journal of Clinical Hypnosis, 17*, 143-157, in Erickson, M.H., & Rossi, E.L. (ed.). (1980). *The collected papers of Milton H. Erickson on hypnosis. Volume I: Nature of hypnosis and suggestion.* New York: Irvington Publishers, Inc., 412-420. Retrieved from http://www.scribd.com/doc/11320394/Erickson-Collected-Papers-Vol1

Gruzelier, J. H. (2006). Frontal functions, connectivity and neural efficiency underpinning hypnosis and hypnotic susceptibility. *Contemporary Hypnosis, 23*(1), 15-32.

Gruzelier, J., Gray, M. & Horn, P. (2002). The involvement of frontally modulated attention in hypnosis and hypnotic susceptibility: Cortical evoked potential evidence. *Contemporary Hypnosis, 19*(4), 179-189.

Schjoedt, U., Stødkilde-Jørgensen, H., Geertz, A.W., Lund, T.E., & Roepstorff, A. (2009). The power of charisma – perceived charisma inhibits the frontal executive network of believers in intercessory prayer. *Social Cognitive and Effective Neuroscience, 4*, 199-207. Retrieved from http://scan.oxfordjournals.org/content/early/2010/03/12/scan.nsq023.full.pdf+html

Stephens, G.J., Silbert, L.J., & Hasson, U. (2010). Speaker–listener neural coupling underlies successful communication. *Proceedings of the National Academy of Sciences, 107*(32), 14425-14430 Retrieved from http://www.pnas.org/content/early/2010/07/13/1008662107.full.pdf+html

Steinbeck, J. (1954) *Sweet Thursday.* New York: Penguin.

# INDEX

# Excerpt from
# *Emotion: The Power of Change*
## *A Science-Based Approach to Ericksonian Hypnosis*

## WHAT IS HYPNOSIS?

The word "hypnotism," coined by Scottish Surgeon Dr. James Braid in 1842, covers a number of phenomena. The word comes from the Greek term for "sleep," although hypnosis does not involve physical sleep. At the most basic level hypnosis is the art of suggestion. Training in hypnosis involves learning to use language in emotionally suggestive ways as a catalyst for profound personal change.

### Levels of Relaxation

One way to look at classic clinical hypnosis is as a relaxation phenomenon. When you are completely awake, alert, and conscious, your brain wave cycles can be up to 20 cycles per second (hertz, or Hz). This is the electric cycle of the brain as measured by an electroencephalograph (EEG) machine. Wide-awake consciousness occurs in a range from 14 to 20 Hz and is called Beta level awareness.

Most of us have had the experience of doing something we really enjoy and losing track of time. We've also had the experience of being stuck trying to solve a problem, make a decision, or do something creative—only to have a Eureka! moment the next morning in the shower. As John Steinbeck said, "It is a common experience that a problem difficult at night is resolved in the morning after the committee of sleep has worked on it" (1954, p. 107). This relaxed, creative state is Alpha level relaxation, at a cycle of 9 to 14 Hz. The hallmarks of Alpha state are creativity and losing track of time. Think about it: Creativity is not a rational process. Creativity occurs when an unconscious part of you sees connections and solutions which you did not see before and you have an "a-ha" experience.

On the other end of the spectrum, true sleep, where you can dream, occurs at 4 Hz or less (down to about 1.5 Hz), and is termed deep Delta sleep.

Between Alpha and Delta is Theta level relaxation, 4 to 9 Hz. Most of us have had the experience of dozing off while watching TV or reading late at night. Anyone seeing you would think you were asleep, but you know you are really not asleep. Think of a husband snoring on the sofa while "watching" a ball game. Theta is the dreamy state of falling asleep (or the luxurious time waking up on a non-rushed morning). In this state, cortisol, the body's primary stress hormone, decreases. Feel-good happy neurotransmitters like beta-endorphins and serotonin increase, providing a wonderful experience. Theta also involves being more emotionally open. Classic clinical hypnosis involves relaxation to this level.

It is important to note that hypnotic language can be used to promote emotional change at any of the levels of consciousness. The great hypnotist and physician Milton Erickson describes hypnotic work in the "ordinary waking state" many times in his writings (cf. Erickson & Rossi, 1975). It is also interesting to note that the word "trance" is used to describe both a relaxed Theta state and an ecstatic and energized upper Beta state (both of which provide experiences outside the normal range of emotional familiarity, and thus create greater suggestibility).

**Deep Relaxation**

The voice in your head that you think of as *you* is called your executive function. The executive function is a function of the prefrontal areas of the frontal lobe (a portion of the brain located just behind the forehead). During sleep, the frontal lobe naturally goes offline. The best way to visualize this may be to think of a light bulb on a dimmer switch slowly dimming down.

Classic relaxed hypnotic suggestibility is associated with frontal inhibition (Gruzelier, Gray, & Horn, 2002; Jamieson, & Sheehan, 2004; Gruzelier, 2006). There is also deactivation of the executive function in the frontal lobe during hypnotic relaxation (Schjoedt, Stødkilde-Jørgensen, Geertz, Lund, & Roepstorff, 2009).

While the frontal lobe naturally relaxes into sleep, other parts of your brain continue to be engaged, of course. This relaxation of the rational or cognitive process of the brain allows hypnotic work to be done at a more emotional level, by engaging more emotional parts of the brain. Since emotions—not information—drive behavior, this relaxation creates a process of change which is more rapid and operates on a deeper level than cognitive changes.

Of course, the more emotional or non-rational parts of you are still you. You are always active in framing and creating changes. Hypnosis is a process for greater self-control. Even a skilled hypnotherapist cannot take you anywhere you do not want to go, but he or she can help you create profound changes that seem out of reach at a conscious level.

**What about Stage or Entertainment Hypnosis?**

Stage work is different from clinical hypnosis, but can involve the same relaxation phenomena. Other processes are also involved in stage work, such as creating compliance, using trivial commitments or "yes sets" to move people into a hypnotic state, and even performance pressure from the audience. Stage hypnotists are also typically interested in finding participants who are very directly suggestible (they relax into hypnosis easily with direct suggestions) and highly physically suggestible (they actually do what is suggested while in the hypnotic state, rather than simply engaging in it as a mental process). None of these factors are significant for clinical hypnosis.

It is important to remember that all hypnotic phenomena rely on a relationship of mutual rapport and trust between the hypnotist and the participant. When someone goes up on a stage, she or he is giving the hypnotist a tremendous amount of psychological permission—that is, the person knows the nature of the show and wants to participate. If your reaction to a stage show is that it is not for you, it is unlikely that you would make a good participant.

In a clinical setting, rapport between the hypnotherapist and the client is critical. Stephens, Silbert, & Hasson (2010) found brain activity aligning between individuals during effective communication—that is, the brain wave patterns of two people having a "great conversation"—tend to become the same.

# ABOUT THE AUTHOR

Dr. Fredric Mau was recognized by his peers with the HypnoScience award for research advancing the profession at the international Hypnosekongress in Zürich, Switzerland, in 2013. He is a frequent, lively and popular presenter on the neuroscience and practice of hypnosis at professional conferences; he frequently teaches continuing education for therapists. Dr. Mau is a licensed professional counselor, a distance-credentialed counselor, a board-certified hypnotherapist, and a certified instructor of hypnosis. His first book, *Emotion: The Power of Change, A Science-Based Approach to Ericksonian Hypnosis*, has delighted professionals and curious general readers as well. For more than a decade, Dr. Mau has helped hundreds of clients successfully create different realities through his private practice in Columbia, South Carolina. His distinctive approach to therapy blends Ericksonian hypnosis, narrative therapy, motivational interviewing, and solution-focused brief therapy. To engage Dr. Mau as a speaker or for therapy, or to provide feedback on this book, please contact him at WatermarkColumbia.com

# ABOUT THE COVER PHOTOGRAPHER

Libby Gamble is an award-winning photographer based in Asheville, NC. She holds a master's degree in the fine arts from the Academy of Art University in San Francisco. While studying there, she was intrigued by the many different shapes, sizes, colors, textures and lines she found in the doors she discovered, and she began to collect their images. Libby remains intrigued by the possibility that lies behind any door-- no matter how it looks from the outside. You can see her work at LibbyGamble.com